TWENTIETH CENTURY
INTERPRETATIONS

MAYNARD MACK, *Series Editor*
Yale University

NOW AVAILABLE
Collections of Critical Essays
ON

THE ADVENTURES OF HUCKLEBERRY FINN

ALL FOR LOVE

ARROWSMITH

AS YOU LIKE IT

THE DUCHESS OF MALFI

THE FROGS

THE GREAT GATSBY

HAMLET

HENRY V

THE ICEMAN COMETH

SAMSON AGONISTES

THE SCARLET LETTER

THE SOUND AND THE FURY

TWELFTH NIGHT

WALDEN

THE WASTE LAND

TWENTIETH CENTURY INTERPRETATIONS
OF

AS YOU LIKE IT

A Collection of Critical Essays

Edited by

JAY L. HALIO

Prentice-Hall, Inc. *Englewood Cliffs, N. J.*

Acknowledgments

I owe thanks to the librarians of the University of Malaya library in Kuala Lumpur, where I began this project, and to the office staff of the Department of English, University of California, Davis, for all their help in assembling the materials I have used. I must also thank the various authors, editors, and publishers for their kind permission to reprint copyrighted work.

Current printing (last number):
10 9 8 7 6 5 4 3 2 1

For Brian and Amy

Contents

Introduction

by Jay L. Halio

In these times of increased emphasis upon education, Orlando's opening complaint in *As You Like It*—that he is not getting enough education—or any at all—must strike a responsive chord. For Sir Rowland de Boys, his father, not only bequeathed his youngest son "poor a thousand crowns," but charged his eldest son, Oliver, "on his blessing" to breed his brother well. The middle son, Jaques, is at school, from whence golden reports come back of his profit; Orlando is kept rustically at home. Chafing at this treatment, Orlando resolves to square matters with his brother or, taking his thousand crowns, to fend for himself. His father's spirit grows strong within him, and he can no longer tolerate the treatment meted out to him.

In the repeated reference to his descent from old Sir Rowland, we become aware of something else bequeathed to Orlando—his innate nobility. If it is this that makes him rise in mutiny against Oliver, it is also this that makes Oliver resent him and resolve to be rid of him. Paradoxically, although Oliver as eldest son inherits his father's lands, Orlando appears to have inherited his father's virtues. "Yet he's gentle; never school'd and yet learned; full of noble device; of all sorts enchantingly beloved," muses Oliver (I. i. 172-4). But whatever his inherent abilities, nature is not enough for Orlando; he will have nurture, too: and this combination of nature and nurture becomes a central thematic concern in *As You Like It*.

The first thing Orlando learns is that a man's own brother may turn against him—even try to have him killed. After he defeats Charles the wrestler, Orlando discovers that Oliver means to continue his hostility and burn down his lodgings. Not all the world loves a winner; Duke Frederick, discovering Orlando's parentage, also turns against him at the very moment of his victory. As old Adam says, "to some kind of men / Their graces serve them but as enemies" (II. iii. 10-11), but Orlando is only now finding this out.

Just as Orlando's virtues are "sanctified and holy traitors" to him, so the whole world seems topsy-turvy when "what is comely / Envenoms him that bears it" (II. iii. 14-15). But some virtues, or the bearers of them, remain constant: by offering up his life's savings as well as his

services to the now outcast Orlando, Adam shows himself to be not of
the fashion of these times, where men willingly enough cut any or all
natural bonds in their lust for money or power. And, despite serious
misgivings, Orlando cannot refuse his generosity. Together, he and
Adam set out on a journey that will eventually take them to the forest
of Arden, the refuge of the banished duke, and to Rosalind.

This is Orlando's first exposure to the wickedness of the world and,
were he to experience an unrelieved exposure to such shocks, he doubt-
less would become an embittered, melancholy man not unlike Jaques,
the duke's courtier. But Orlando is not Jaques any more than Jaques
is Shakespeare's spokesman in the play, however much certain nine-
teenth-century critics misunderstood this role. Jaques, like many of the
characters in *As You Like It,* offers only a partial view, seriously in
need of the kinds of qualification that others, pre-eminently Rosalind,
give it. The total point of view of the play is a composite of such
counterbalancing views, not any single view, unless that view is Rosalind's, which represents, as we shall see, a properly balanced outlook.

It is perhaps for this reason, or one like it, that Shakespeare does not
make the trip to Arden too easy. "O Jupiter, how weary are my spirits!"
exclaims Rosalind as she arrives; and Adam is almost dead of hunger
and fatigue as Orlando helps to carry him in. Whatever the special
properties of the forest—and they are many—it requires considerable
effort to get there. The effort, of course, is at one level the effort of
the imagination; for in this forest of Arden we find not only the
Warwickshire milkmaid Audrey and her homespun William, but the
storybook characters Silvius and Phebe, and even Hymen, the god of
marriage.

Clearly, the forest is also the traditional retreat, or haven, of the
oppressed. It is not entirely without dangers, if natural ones, such as
winter and rough weather, snakes and wild animals. And like any university, it is an ideal place for learning: a place for the imagination to
wander in, reasonably well protected from the worst disasters that may
occur, but not so cut off from reality as to foster too disabling a sense of
security. Here, apart from "sermons in stones," one may hear lectures
on "Time's paces," forms of melancholy, and seven degrees of "the lie."
A man may learn to woo a maid, and wed her here; but he must spend
his life married to her elsewhere, unless he can fold himself up into
the pages from which Silvius and Phebe emerge (and, presumably, to
which they return). Here, also, Orlando may be compelled to wrestle
with his conscience and commit himself to a moral choice between
vengeance or mercy in saving his brother from a starved lioness. Happily—for unlike *Hamlet,* this is a comedy—Orlando makes the right
choice and lets his innate nobility win over his "just occasion." Impor-

tant as it is, however, this is neither the first nor the last of Orlando's victories.

The central episodes of the play, after all, focus directly upon the love relationship between Orlando and Rosalind. Although they have met and fallen in love in the world of Duke Frederick and his court, their love could hardly be expected to flourish in that noxious environment; hence another reason for their arrival in Arden. Rosalind's disguise as Ganymede, originally adopted for other motives, now serves as a means through which she may educate her lover in the proper attitudes to love. At first surprised to find Orlando in the forest, then somewhat disappointed that this appearance as a lover matches neither his verse nor his protestations, Rosalind begins roundly to take him in hand. Enumerating the distinguishing marks of a lover (III. ii. 392 ff.), she concludes that Orlando is rather too "point-device" in his accoutrements; but eventually she convinces herself that he does love her. At that point, or during Orlando's wooing of Ganymede-Rosalind, her job changes. She must now educate Orlando away from the excesses of romantic love into which he is tending, and develop in him a deeper yet nonetheless devoted response. This she accomplishes in part by exposing love's follies, by recounting the real nature of men and women in love, and in general by impressing upon Orlando the necessity for keeping his wits about him, even in love, as she herself does. Their common attitude toward love, and to each other, emerges finally as one that, compared with those of the other "country copulatives," augurs best for an enduring relationship.

Nor is Orlando the only one thus educated in the play; in fact, the dramatic structure may be grasped in one way by understanding the play's basic techniques of parallel and parody. If Rosalind and Orlando represent the best balanced attitude toward love, this attitude has been defined for us in part by the relationships of other lovers. At the one extreme are Silvius and Phebe, the lovers of pastoral tradition, whose antics Shakespeare here satirizes principally through the device of having Phebe fall in love with the disguised Rosalind. But Rosalind also directly mocks Silvius's excesses of language and action when, for example, she very precisely describes Phebe's actual features in contrast to those attributed to her by her so cruelly mistreated lover (III. v. 35 ff.). Orlando, especially when he turns to hanging verses upon trees, bids fair to run into the same sorts of excesses until Rosalind checks him. A main function of Silvius and Phebe in the play, then, is to reveal how the conventions and other artificialities, or stereotypes, of the Petrarchan love tradition (made enormously popular in England by Elizabethan sonneteers) may subvert an otherwise basically sound initial emotion. Elsewhere, in his Sonnet 130, Shakespeare adopts a similar attitude toward this Petrarchanism, which he again uses as a counterpoise to a more sincere expression of real love.

At the opposite extreme from Silvius and Phebe, and therefore no closer to a balanced approach (although they help to define that approach), are Touchstone and Audrey. A most earthy wench, Audrey seems as ready as Touchstone to get through any kind of marriage ceremony if it will expedite what is apparently for both of them the real business of love—sex. Only the timely intervention of spoilsport Jaques prevents Sir Oliver Martext from joining these two in what would be, in every sense, a false match. Audrey has not wit nor language nor manners to equal Touchstone's, any more than does William, from whom Touchstone steals her quite openly; but she has just enough ambition to become "a woman of the world," that is, to desire with all her heart any kind of union with the court jester (V. iii. 3-5). Touchstone, on his part, knows well enough what he is about, but neither his clear-sightedness nor frank confession ("man hath his desires") should blind us to his partial attitude toward love.

Between these extremes of literary attitudinizing and downright physical crudity is the better balanced view of Rosalind, which takes account of both impulses. However deeply in love she is with Orlando —and her frequent admissions to Celia are certain evidence of the fact —she never lets emotion entirely overmaster her when they are together. But neither, of course, does she seek to stifle emotion altogether. This theme of properly attuning strong feelings and good sense thus explains why Shakespeare carefully alternates the various lovers' appearances in the forest. Beginning with Rosalind's first moments in Arden, her feelings are immediately paralleled by Silvius's love-lament to Corin, which is in turn parodied by Touchstone's reminiscence of Jane Smile—one of poor Audrey's predecessors.

The relationship between Celia and Oliver, the fourth of the country couples, is much less fully developed; in fact, it is scarcely developed at all, except for Rosalind's account of how the two fell in love at first sight and made "a pair of stairs to marriage, which they will climb incontinent, or else be incontinent before marriage" (V. ii. 42-4). But Shakespeare, as we know from other plays as well as this one, took a dim view of premarital "incontinence": in his last play, *The Tempest,* Prospero gives strict orders on this subject to Ferdinand and Miranda, who are thus left to spin out the time until their nuptials playing chess. In any event, Orlando consents to Oliver's wish to be married straightaway (though why Oliver feels the need to get this consent from a younger brother is unexplained, unless we understand that, after his "rebirth," Oliver turns to his deliverer as to an elder). By his real change in character, Oliver has earned no less a prize than a duke's daughter—and deserves her all the more because he knows her so far only as "Aliena." Besides, he has already abandoned to Orlando all claims upon their father's estate, and seems content to "live and die a shepherd" (V. ii. 6-14). Celia, for her part, has served her function as the voice of wit and reason during Rosalind's transports of love; it is now her turn to be similarly transported, although dramatically there is no need to extend the situation more than Shakespeare does. It is quite enough to bring this couple to the marriage altar along with the rest. Their betrothal is in fact the precipitant cause for erecting the altar; and the appropriate point of view toward love has by this time been well enough established, certainly for the audience, whatever the case may be for Oliver and Celia.

II

The system of parallels and contrasts, so important in developing the attitude toward love set forth again, is used to promote other ramifications of theme or plot in *As You Like It*. In contrast to the two sets of brothers in the play, Rosalind and Celia, mere cousins, enjoy a relationship "whose loves / Are dearer than the natural bond of sisters" (I. ii. 286-7). Far from the greed that makes Frederick usurp his brother's dukedom, or the jealousy that sets Oliver against Orlando, Celia is so devoted to her cousin that at the moment of Rosalind's banishment she resolves to give up everything—father, court, and all— to go along with her. Indeed, it is Celia who first suggests going to Arden to join her banished uncle, and answers Rosalind's fears by suggesting that they go in disguise.

In the forest itself, William's bumpkinish ways strikingly contrast with the manners of Silvius, but it is Corin rather than either of them who represents the best model of rural life. He quite holds his own, moreover, against Touchstone's "courtly" wit which, upon close inspection, proves to be little more, here, than tricky equivocation. Wearied more than he is vanquished, Corin tries to put an end to their encounter with a quite reasonable statement of his position: "Sir, I am a true labourer; I earn that I eat, get that I wear; owe no man hate, envy no man's happiness; glad of other men's good, content with my harm; and the greatest of my pride is to see my ewes graze and my lambs suck" (III. ii. 77-81). Whatever Corin lacks in ambition—and in Shakespeare's day to be content, like Adam and Corin, was a virtue —he more than makes up in good sense; but it is on none of these grounds that Touchstone continues the attack, more intent as he is on the exercise of his wit than on anything else. Touchstone is a true courtier in this regard; and only the entrance of Rosalind stops him, or rather, deflects the point of his attack from Corin's livelihood to Orlando's verses.

However fit Arden may be for men like Corin, or however useful for others as a temporary refuge, Shakespeare does not sentimentalize his vision of pastoral life: it is not a fit place for all men all the time. Duke Senior's opening speech (II. i) establishes the point. "Sweet are the uses of adversity"; and the good duke, we may infer, learns a great deal from his forced exile. But he does not lose sight of the fact that it *is* exile; it is, in short, "adversity"—not his proper home, not the one he most desires under all circumstances. The most we can say— the most the duke says, if we interpret him correctly—is that he is making the best of a bad situation. He neither complains like Touchstone, whose first and lasting impression is summed up by his remark, "Now am I in Arden, the more fool I" (II. iv. 16), nor exaggerates like Jaques, who carries to extremes the duke's humane compassion for hunted deer (II. i. 21 ff.), and elsewhere is exposed as something of a hypocrite (II. vii. 64-9) or a fool (IV. i. 1-29). Thus Rosalind's balanced judgment is but a step from that displayed by her father.

III

Although *As You Like It* was not published until Heminges and Condell, Shakespeare's fellow actors and shareholders, collected his works for the great Folio of 1623 (some seven years after their colleague's death), we are reasonably certain that the play as we have it was acted just before the end of the sixteenth century. It is not among the plays Francis Meres mentions in *Palladis Tamia* (1598), but on August 4, 1600 it was entered in the *Stationers' Register* along with three other Shakespearean plays "to be staied." These facts together with an evaluation of the play's style and characterization have led most scholars to place *As You Like It* with Shakespeare's other mature comedies, *Much Ado About Nothing* and *Twelfth Night,* in the so-called "joyous" group. Certainly Rosalind's prose is every bit as supple and witty as Beatrice's in *Much Ado;* and either heroine would be a fit match for Falstaff in *Henry IV,* written just previously. Nevertheless, some commentators, following J. Dover Wilson's textual analysis, date the play much earlier, to 1593, and consider the Folio text a later revision. Certainly, the pastoral motif reappears intermittently throughout Shakespeare's career. As early as *The Two Gentlemen of Verona* (c. 1592) Shakespeare had dramatized the situation of banished gentlemen forced to lived like Robin Hood of old; and varieties of pastoralism recur in the last plays. But it is especially in *As You Like It* that

Shakespeare subjects pastoralism to satirical techniques of handling, a point that may have something to do both with his own mood at the time (if we accept the plays, mentioned above, as written just before or after this one), and with his reaction to the excesses of his contemporaries, who by the end of the century had produced an immense volume of pastoral literature. Anthologies of verse became more frequent after the success of Tottel's *Miscellany* (1557); but it is especially significant, perhaps, that in 1600 an anthology exclusively composed of pastoral poetry, *England's Helicon,* was first published. Coincidentally, it was entered in the *Stationers' Register* on the same day as *As You Like It.* Shakespeare's play probably did little to stem the outflow of pastoral poetry or pastoral drama: the Children of Queen Elizabeth's Chapel performed Ben Jonson's *Cynthia's Revels* late in 1600, and at Court on January 6, 1601; a translation of *Il Pastor Fido* appeared soon afterward, and Samuel Daniel's *The Queen's Arcadia* in 1605. And by 1614 a newly augmented edition of *England's Helicon* had been published. But *As You Like It* must surely have given the more thoughtful Elizabethans—as it must give us—some food for thought, a fresher outlook, perhaps, even as it entertains.

That it was not published in quarto form, but was entered in the *Stationers' Register* expressly to prevent unauthorized publication, is taken by some scholars as proof positive that the play was still drawing well at the Globe by mid-1600. But we ought to remember that the fact of early publication (or its absence) in itself proves nothing. Some of the most popular of Shakespeare's plays, such as *Hamlet,* managed to find their way into print with or without the players' permission; and *Much Ado About Nothing,* entered in the *Register* of the Stationers' Company along with *As You Like It,* at the same time and for the same purpose, was authorized for publication a few weeks later and appeared in quarto by the end of the year.

The change of mind concerning the authorization for publication of *Much Ado* may possibly be related to a change in the actors who comprised the Lord Chamberlain's Men. Certainly, the difference between the clowns in *Much Ado* (Dogberry) and *As You Like It* (Touchstone) and *Twelfth Night* (Feste) is partly the result of Robert Armin's replacing Will Kempe in the acting company. With little hope of reviving *Much Ado* after Kempe's departure, the players may have decided to get what they could from the printed version of the play, while the other two "joyous" comedies still held the boards.

But it is easy to make too much of such impingements upon the dramatist's imagination, just as too much used to be made of Shakespeare's inserting "food for the groundlings" in his plays. Whatever the exigencies of his immediate practical situation, Shakespeare was able to utilize his resources—literary materials such as Lodge's *Rosa-*

lynde, the physical properties of his theater, or the talents of his company—and to fuse them in the creation of a new dramatic and poetic unity. It is obvious that if Lodge had never written his novel, Shakespeare would never have written this play; he probably would have written something else, which could just as well have been given the same title and might even have contained similar motifs. As a practicing dramatist and a principal shareholder in his company, Shakespeare had to produce plays and, until later in his career, even act in them (he was once thought to have acted old Adam in *As You Like It*). This much is certain, and—to put an end to further speculation—so is the existence of the play, which it is our pleasure as well as our right to understand as it has come down to us, however and whenever it may have been conceived and produced. To this end, the collection of critical essays that follows is devoted; but it cannot be overemphasized that they are in no way a substitute for the play itself.

PART ONE

Interpretations

Shakespearian Comedy: "The Consummation"

by H. B. Charlton

. . . To see these plays as a form of comedy, it is perhaps easiest to begin by realizing that in kind they are essentially and obviously different from traditional classical comedy. Their main characters arouse admiration; they excite neither scorn nor contempt. They inspire us to be happy with them; they do not merely cajole us into laughing at them. Therein lies the fundamental difference between classical and Shakespearian comedy. Classical comedy is conservative. It implies a world which has reached stability sufficient for itself. Its members are assumed to be fully aware of the habits and the morals which preserve an already attained state of general well-being. The main interest is the exposure of offenders against common practice and against unquestioned propriety in the established fitness of things. Hence, its manner is satire, and its standpoint is public common sense. But Shakespearian comedy is a more venturesome and a more imaginative undertaking. It does not assume that the conditions and the requisites of man's welfare have been certainly established, and are therefore a sanctity only to be safeguarded. It speculates imaginatively on modes, not of preserving a good already reached, but of enlarging and extending the possibilities of this and other kinds of good. Its heroes (or heroines, to give them the dues of their sex) are voyagers in pursuit of a happiness not yet attained, a brave new world wherein man's life may be fuller, his sensations more exquisite, and his joys more widespread, more lasting, and so more humane. But as the discoverer reaches this higher bliss, he (or rather she) is making his conquests in these realms of the spirit accessible not only to himself but to all others in whom he has inspired the same way of apprehending existence. He has not merely preserved the good which was; he has refined, varied, and widely extended it. Hence Shakespearian comedy is not finally satiric; it is poetic. It is not con-

"Shakespearian Comedy: '*The Consummation.*'" *From Chapter IX of* Shakespearian Comedy *by H. B. Charlton (London: Methuen & Company Ltd., 1938), pp. 277-83. Copyright 1938 by Methuen & Company, Ltd. Reprinted by permission of the publisher.*

servative; it is creative. The way of it is that of the imagination rather
than that of pure reason. It is an artist's vision, not a critic's exposition.

But though the ultimate world of Shakespeare's comedy is romantic,
poetic, and imaginative, it is by no means unsubstantial and fantastic.
The forest of Arden is no conventional Arcadia. Its inhabitants are not
exempt from the penalty of Adam. Winter, rough weather, the sea-
son's differences, the icy fang and churlish chiding of the winter's wind
invade Arden as often as they invade this hemisphere of ours. Nor does
manna fall to it from heaven. One may come by a sufficient sustenance
of flesh, if one has the weapons and the impulse to make a breach in
the conventionality of idyllic Nature by killing its own creatures, the
deer, to whom the forest is the assigned and native dwelling place.
Arden, too, is not ignorant of the earthly landlordism which cramps
the laborers' life with harshness:

> My master is of churlish disposition
> And little recks to find the way to heaven
> By doing deeds of hospitality.

And, after all, pastoral life in Arden is merely episodic in the round of
man's fuller existence: "when I was at home, I was in a better place."
Rosalind and Orlando will return to live their adult life in the society
of man and in a civilization which will impose on them the duties of
extended social responsibilities. Only by hearsay is life in Arden
reputed to be a fleeting the time carelessly as they did in the golden
age; even young Orlando knows that it may be a losing and a neglect-
ing of the creeping hours. Arden, indeed, may properly excite the witti-
cisms of Touchstone by its rusticities; it may arouse the twisted senti-
mentalism of Jaques by its Darwinian illustrations of the cruel struggle
for survival.

But Arden survives. It survives as an immeasurable enlargement of
the universe of comedy. No longer is the comic spirit confined to the
city and to the marketplace. And not only is there Arden. There is
Illyria. There are the vast expanses of a less known world—romantic
countries on whose coasts all the strange and stirring episodes that man
has dreamed may come true: shipwreck, piracy, warfare, marvelous
escapes from imminent death, hazards boldly and even recklessly encountered. Or, may be, lands of *dolce far niente,* where music is the
food of love, where corporeal and material exigencies offer no impedi-
ment to man's grasp at the opulence of a merely sentimental existence.
In such a climate, a duke may wallow orientally in the luxuriance of
sheer sensuous excitement: but, in the same air, the witchcraft of adventure will strike from a simple ship's captain a nobility of benevolence
which will sacrifice all for another's good.

"This is the air, this is the glorious sun." But it is not only in its geographical atmosphere that the world of these comedies is so vastly larger than that of classical comedy, so much more radiant than that of Shakespeare's earlier romantic comedies, and so much more rich than that of Falstaff's Eastcheap. In its own turn, the world of the spirit has been equally extended. As one obvious sign of it, man has become more exquisitely conscious of music. Of course, there has always been a human impulse for caterwauling; and, in their cups, men have commonly felt themselves to be such dogs at a catch that they could rouse the night owl and make the welkin dance. But it is in these great plays that men are suddenly brought up against the stupendous and apparently incredibly foolish circumstance that sheep's guts are potent to hale the souls out of their bodies.

There had, of course, always been music in Elizabethan plays. It was hallowed by their earliest tradition. In daily life, too, an Elizabethan, whether nobleman or peasant, had found music as much an habitual part of his occupation as was eating or drinking or working.

> O, fellow, come, the song we had last night.
> Mark it, Cesario, it is old and plain;
> The spinsters and the knitters in the sun
> And the free maids that weave their thread with bones
> Do use to chant it.

It is not only that song and music irradiate these plays—the very clown of one of them has almost lost his clownage to qualify as a singer—the important point is that the men and women of the play, and Shakespeare and his audience, are becoming conscious of what the spell of music implies. "That strain again"; these old and antique songs were apt to arouse amorousness in Orsino and yet "to relieve him of his passion much." To recognize the palpable effect of music was the first step: to become aware of its implications was another. In men's secular lives, music ministered most powerfully to their passion of love. "If music be the food of love, play on." And so they found themselves at the very heart of the mystery, the recognition that, however strange, sheep's guts did in fact hale their souls out of their bodies. They were feelingly aware that the soul is susceptible to strange and unaccountable impulses, and that, responding to them, it enters a rich and novel spiritual kingdom.

What this means for the purposes of Shakespearian comedy is this. Man had discovered that he was a much less rational and a much more complex creature than he had taken himself to be. His instincts and his intuitions, his emotions and his moods were as real and as distinctive a part of him as his reason and his plain common sense. They were, in fact, a much more incalculable yet often a much more exciting and satisfying part of his nature than was his sober intellect. Man was rediscovering the validity of his intuitions and of his emotions; he was, in particular, and for the express purposes of comedy, becoming intellectually aware that the tumultuous condition of his being which followed his falling in love and urged him on to woo, was in fact no mean and mainly physical manifestation of his personality; it was, in fact, the awakening in him of the fuller capacities of his spirit.

So, amongst the themes of Elizabethan comedy, love had now justified its primacy. It had willy nilly always been the major interest. But, as the earlier comedies have shown, its usurpations had been hazardous for the spirit of comedy. It had hitherto forced itself into a Pyrrhic triumph as an alien invader backed only by the forces of popular preference. It could now rightly take its place in Elizabethan comedy as the recognized presiding genius. It was the touchstone by which fine spirits were struck to their finest issues. It was also, of course, a test by which weaker mortals revealed their weakness, grosser ones their grossness, and foolish ones their folly. It is noteworthy, however, that though these three great comedies are even more exclusively the plays of lovers and their wooing than are the earlier ones, seldom does Shakespeare allow their wooing to express itself through the full gamut of its lyric modulations. Its utterance is adapted to a dramatic, and, indeed, to a comic scene: depth of affection is displayed rather by hints and by deeds than by the conventional phrase of the love poet. The homily of love from its gentle pulpiters is felt to be tedious, and is seldom allowed to weary its hearers. Often, indeed, when the wooing itself is an extended episode of the story, it is camouflaged in circumstances shaped by the wooers to cover their real passion. Beatrice and Benedick deliberately adopt a kind of inverted technique of lovemaking; and for them, the normal idiom of lovers is feigned by others so as to be overheard by the two who are to be the victims of the device. Rosalind, disguised as Ganymede, pretends to be herself in order to teach Orlando to woo. Viola expresses her own love only by innuendo, and finds a sort of outlet for her inhibition, as well as a gratification for her own sense of restraint, in unfolding to Olivia the passion of the Duke's love, as if hallooing her name to the reverberate hills to make the babbling gossip of the air cry out "Olivia." But having done this, Viola will find it easier to be her natural self. "I took great pains to study it, and 'tis poetical." In the throes of her own love, she will revert to sanity.

Indeed, deeply as these heroines fall in love, no person in the plays is more aware of the follies into which love may delude its victims. It is Rosalind who reproves the foolish shepherd Silvius for following Phebe like foggy south puffing with wind and rain:

> 'tis such fools as you
> That make the world full of ill-favoured children.

But she will advise silly giddy-brained Phebe to go down on her knees and thank heaven, fasting for a good man's love. Lunacy and love are yet not entirely different diseases. "Love is merely a madness, and, I tell you, deserves as well a dark house and a whip as madmen do: and the reason why they are not so punished and cured is, that the lunacy is so ordinary that the whippers are in love too." Madness, but inevitable madness: and a madness in which the visions are a mingling of revelation and of hallucination. Who shall know which is which? Who better than the one who knows most of the frequency of hallucination? Rosalind is well aware of what may be falsely claimed for love, so well aware that she can make mock of the possibilities: "the poor world is almost six thousand years old, and in all this time there was not any man died in his own person, videlicet, in a love cause. Troilus had his brains dashed out with a Grecian club; yet he did what he could to die before, and he is one of the patterns of love. Leander, he would have lived many a fair year, though Hero had turned nun, if it had not been for a hot midsummer night; for, good youth, he went but forth to wash him in the Hellespont and being taken with the cramp was drowned: and the foolish chroniclers of that age found it was 'Hero of Sestos.' But these are all lies: men have died from time to time and worms have eaten them, but not for love." Yet there is no wrestling with Rosalind's affections, when they take the part of the man with whom she has fallen desperately and suddenly in love.

Rosalind, Viola, and, to a less extent, Beatrice, are Shakespeare's images of the best way of love. They, and the men in whom they inspire love, are Shakespeare's representation of the office of love to lift mankind to a richer life. So, by the entry into it of love, not only has the world of these comedies become a bigger world: the men and women who inhabit it have become finer and richer representatives of human nature. They have entered into the possession of spiritual endowments which, if hitherto suspected to exist at all, had either been distrusted as dangerous or had become moribund through desuetude. They have claimed the intuitive, the subconscious, and the emotional as instruments by which personality may bring itself into a fuller consciousness of and a completer harmony with the realities of existence. They have left Theseus far behind; they have also outgrown Falstaff. . . .

The Use of Comedy in *As You Like It*

by C. L. Barber

Most criticism of Shakespeare's comedy has been impressionistic and appreciative rather than analytical. Since there is plenty to be serious about in the tragedies, critics have made it a virtue to be gay and glancing about "creatures of the woods and wilds." There has been sustained critical discussion only in connection with Falstaff and the problem comedies. The consequence of such spotty treatment has been to make the comedy appear casual and miscellaneous. Shakespeare did indeed write a great many different kinds of comedy, and often in a happy-go-lucky spirit that produced plays relatively loosely organized. Actually, however, we can repeatedly see in his works a method, not in the least casual, of using humor as an element in a larger, serious dramatic whole; and we can find in this method the organizing principles, not of all his comedy, but of his best comedy. In connection with the humor in the tragedies, aspects of this use of comedy have been described in terms of comic relief. But the method is not confined to the tragedies; and comic relief has too often been taken to mean that the humor serves merely to divert the audience from serious matters, so that anything funny would do. In reality the finest comedy is not a diversion from serious themes but an alternative mode of developing them: not only the placing of the humor but also its content is determined by its function in the whole play. A close examination of the way the comedy functions in one of the plays where it is most successfully used can perhaps define principles of dramatic construction which will have a general application in discriminating between casual and motivated humor, and between those plays where comic and serious material are organically united and those where Shakespeare fell back on the formula of throwing in a little of both.

As You Like It is a good choice for this purpose because it is one of the plays which appear at first glance most casual. A good way to begin is to ask the simple but much-begged question "What is the comedy

"*The Use of Comedy in* As You Like it," *by C. L. Barber. From* Philological Quarterly, *XXI (1942), 353-67. Reprinted by permission of the author and* Philological Quarterly.

in *As You Like It* about? What does Shakespeare ridicule?" At times
one gets the impression that it doesn't matter very much what the characters make fun of so long as they make fun. The wit seems directed
almost at random, not criticism by laughter, but a buoyant sort of
game, high spirits overflowing in high jinks with language. Certainly
we cannot find the point of the humor in satire; it does not cut into the
real world of Elizabethan men and manners. If we look for social satire
in *As You Like It,* all we find are a few set pieces about such stock
figures as the traveller and the duelist. And these figures seem to be
included rather to exploit their extravagance than to rebuke their
folly. Jaques, in response to a topical interest at the time when the play
appeared, talks a good deal about satire, and proposes to "cleanse the
foul body of th' infected world" with the fool's medicine of ridicule.
But neither Jaques, the amateur fool, nor Touchstone, the professional,
ever really gets around to doing the satirist's work of ridiculing life as
it is, "deeds, and language, such as men do use." After all, they are in
Arden, not in Jonson's London: the infected body of the world is far
away, out of range.

What they make fun of instead is what they can find in Arden—
pastoral innocence and romantic love, life as it might be rather than
life as it is. And this is true throughout the play.; When the comedy is
examined with an eye to what it is about, we find that by far the
greater portion of it is not really introduced at random, but ridicules
precisely the sentiments and behavior which are expressed or represented seriously in the play as a whole.; The play as a whole is not
comic, though we call it a comedy; the comical matter is a mocking
accompaniment to a serious action, romantic and pastoral in character,
which enlists our sympathetic participation.; Touchstone's affair with
Audrey, to mention the most obvious case in point, is a burlesque of
the other love affairs. As a preliminary example of the way the comedy
mocks the serious action, recall his famous remarks to the good duke,
when he comes on with Audrey to take his grotesque part in the multiple marriage: "I press in here, sir, amongst the rest of the country
copulatives, to swear and to forswear, according as marriage binds and
blood breaks." This baldly reduces the pastoral lovers, with their high-
flown sentiments of devotion, to "country copulatives." And Touchstone suggests, by his pat antithesis, that the eternal faith they pledge
is nonsense, that blood will surely break what marriage binds. Yet
these lines are spoken just after the audience has heard, and heard
sympathetically, the lovers' protestations, and just before romantic
faith reaches full tide in the finale of marriage.

This practice of making fun of something which is presented seriously a moment before or a moment after is standard throughout the
play. It raises the question whether the play is divided against itself.

But the humor is not really critical of the ideals on which the serious
action is founded: its contribution is of a different kind. Touchstone's
remarks make fun of the ideal of marriage, not as a bad ideal, but as an
ideal which life does not live up to. His humor thus expresses the difference between the ideal existence represented in the play and life as
a whole, which so frequently is not ideal. The fool is throughout a
representative of the side of human nature which runs counter to the
idyllic and romantic. As another example, consider the attitude he
takes towards pastoral contentment and simplicity. The pastoral ideal
envisages the possibility of enjoying at once the advantages of sophistication and of simplicity. The heroes of Renaissance pastoral, such as
the banished duke in *As You Like It,* can have the best of both worlds,
court and country, because they have a special sort of aristocratic
humility, compounded of many simples, Stoic and Christian. They are
not attached to pomp and are ready to endure loss of status and
physical privations for the sake of innocence, security and sweet-fellow-
ship:

> Happy is your Grace
> That can translate the stubbornness of Fortune
> Into so quiet and so sweet a style.

Touchstone has not this idealized nature: at least, he assumes for the
sake of mockery the role of a discontented exile from the court when
he discusses pastoral content with the shepherd Corin:

> *Corin.* And how like you this shepherd's life, Master Touchstone?
> *Touchstone.* Truly, shepherd, in respect of itself, it is a good life; but in
> respect that it is a shepherd's life, it is naught. In respect that it is soli-
> tary, I like it very well; but in respect that it is private, it is a very vile
> life. Now in respect it is in the fields, it pleaseth me well; but in respect
> it is not in the court, it is tedious. As it is a spare life, look you, it fits
> my humour well; but as there is no more plenty in it, it goes much
> against my stomach.

Under the apparent nonsense of his self-contradictions, Touchstone
penetrates to the contradictory nature of the desires ideally resolved
by pastoral life, to be at once at court and in the fields, to enjoy both
the fat advantages of rank and the spare advantages of the mean and
sure estate. The humor goes to the heart of the pastoral convention
and shows how very clearly Shakespeare understood it. He did not, like
so many romantic writers, mistake its charm for fact. But Touchstone's
remarks clearly do not constitute a criticism of the ideal as such: instead, they imply that the ideal is ideal, that an important phase of
human nature runs counter to it. Their presence in the play thus makes
for an inclusive objectivity concerning its serious theme.

This comic method is precisely the reverse of satire. The satirist presents life as it is and ridicules it because it is not ideal, as we would like it to be and as it should be. Shakespeare goes the other way about: he represents or evokes ideal life, and then makes fun of it because it does not square with life as it ordinarily is. Similar comic presentation of what is not ideal in man is characteristic of medieval fool humor, where the humorist, by his gift of long ears to the long-robed dignitaries, makes the point that, despite their official perfection, they are human too, that *"stultorum numerus infinitus est."* A gulf separates such humor from modern satire, for its basic affirmation is not man's possible perfection but his certain imperfection. It was a function of the pervasively formal and ideal cast of medieval culture, where what should be was more present to the mind than what is: the humorists' natural recourse was to burlesque the pageant of perfection, presenting it as a procession of fools, in crowns, mitres, caps and gowns. Shakespeare's affinities in comedy are medieval rather than modern. Not that his point of view was medieval—his ideal was very different. But his plays are primarily concerned with giving form to ideal life, whether romantic or heroic; and his comedy is a response, a countermovement, to this artistic idealization, as medieval burlesque was a response to the ingrained idealism of the culture. He is always primarily concerned with man's possible perfection; his comic figures, who, in Aristotle's formula, represent men as worse than they are, are almost always foils to ideal personages: even Falstaff, domineering as he became to Justice Shallow, began life, and lived most humorously, as a foil to Prince Hal. For this kind of comedy is by nature an accompaniment, achieving its greatest effects by humorously modifying and controlling our attitude towards dominant serious themes.

The comedy consequently implies a point of vantage outside the serious action, as the humorous tone of a seriously couched remark implies a detached valuation by the speaker of what he is saying. In *As You Like It,* where the serious material is particularly fragile, founded on ideals elaborated by literature rather than by society as a whole, the action is never out of humorous perspective for very long. Rosalind's sense of humor is the principal comic agency; but the detachment fundamental to the comedy is most obvious in Touchstone and Jaques, whose whole function is to be its vehicles. Once or twice these mockers seem to stand altogether outside the play, as when Jaques responds to Orlando's romantic greeting: "Good day and happiness, dear Rosalind!" with "Nay then, God b'wi' you, and you talk in blank verse!"

Although both Jaques and Touchstone are connected with the action well enough at the level of plot, their real position is generally mediate between the audience and the play. Jaques's factitious melan-

choly, which critics have made too much of as a "psychology," serves
primarily to set him at odds with Arden and so motivate a "contem-
plative" mockery from outside. Touchstone is put outside by his
special status as a fool. As a fool, incapable, at least for professional
purposes, of doing anything right, he is beyond the pale of normal
achievements. In anything he tries to do he is comically disabled, as,
for example, in falling in love. All he achieves is a burlesque of love.
And yet, just because he is an outcast, he has none of the illusions
of those who try to be ideal, and so is in a position to make a business
of being dryly objective. "Call me not fool," he says, "till heaven hath
sent me fortune." Heaven sends him Audrey instead, "an ill-favour'd
thing, sir, but mine own,"—not a mistress to generate illusions. In *As
You Like It* the court fool for the first time takes over the work of comic
commentary and burlesque from the clown of the earlier plays; in
Jaques's praise of Touchstone and the corrective virtues of fooling,
Shakespeare can be heard crowing with delight at his discovery.
The figure of the jester, with his recognized social role and rich
traditional meaning, enabled the dramatist to embody in a character
and his relations with other characters the relation of his comic to
his serious action, to make explicit the comedy's purpose of maintaining objectivity. The fact that Shakespeare created both Jaques
and Touchstone out of whole cloth, adding them to the story as it
appears in Lodge's *Rosalynde,* is the best index to what he did in
dramatizing the prose romance. Lodge, though he has a light touch,
treats the idyllic material at face value. He never makes fun of its
assumptions, but stays safely within the convention, because he has
no securely grounded attitude towards it, not being sure of its relation
to reality. Shakespeare scarcely changes the story at all; but where
in Lodge it is presented in the flat, he brings alive the dimension of
its relation to life as a whole. The control of this dimension makes
his version solid as well as delicate.

Indeed, the manipulation of our attitude towards the imagined
conditions of life becomes more important than the plot which un-
rolls under those conditions. The best analogies for the play's structure are in music. *As You Like It* is composed in two movements, of
about equal length, the first developing the pastoral theme, the second
the romantic. Since the essence of pastoral is to feel the country,
not as it is in itself, but in contrast to the court, the first half of
the play is poised around this contrast, moving from the opening
statement of jealousy and conflict to a resolution in the freedom of
Arden. The smaller units of the action recapitulate the same movement from tension to release. A revealing example of the dominance
of this rhythm of feeling is Orlando's entrance, sword in hand, to
interrupt the duke's gracious banquet by a threatening demand for

food. Such behavior on his part is quite out of character (in Lodge he is most courteous); but his brandishing entrance gives Shakespeare occasion to resolve the attitude of struggle once again, this time by a lyric invocation of "what 'tis to pity and be pitied." When this recurrent rhythm has brought us securely into the golden world, and its limitations, in their turn, have been suggested by the humor of Jaques and Touchstone, the pastoral motif as such drops into the background; Rosalind finds Orlando's verses in the second scene of Act III, and the rest of the play elaborates the theme of love. This second movement is like a theme and variations. The love affairs of the three pairs of lovers, Silvius and Phebe and Touchstone and Audrey, as well as the hero and heroine, succeed one another in the easy-going sequence of scenes, while the dramatist deftly plays each off against the others. In each case the humor lies in making us aware of a version of the incongruity between the reality of love and the illusions (in poetry, the hyperboles) which it creates and by which it is expressed. The comic variations are centered around the seriously felt love of Rosalind and Orlando. The final effect is to enhance the reality of this love by making it independent of illusions, whose incongruity with life is recognized and laughed off. We can see this at closer range by examining each affair in turn.

All-suffering Silvius and his tyrannical little Phebe are a bit of Lodge's version taken over, outwardly intact, and set in a wholly new perspective. A "courting eglogue" between them, in the mode of Lodge, is exhibited almost as a formal spectacle, with Corin for presenter and Rosalind and Celia for audience. It is announced as

a pageant truly play'd
Between the pale complexion of true love
And the red glow of scorn and proud disdain.

What we then watch is played "truly"—according to the best current convention: Silvius, employing a familiar gambit, asks for pity; Phebe refuses to believe in love's invisible wound, with exactly the literal-mindedness about the reality of hyperbole which the sonneteers imputed to their mistresses. In Lodge's version, the unqualified Petrarchan sentiments of the pair are presented as valid and admirable. Shakespeare lets us feel the charm of the form; but then he has Rosalind break up their pretty pageant. She reminds them that they are nature's creatures, and that love's purposes are contradicted by too absolute a cultivation of romantic liking or loathing: "I must tell you friendly in your ear, Sell when you can! you are not for all markets." Her exaggerated downrightness humorously underscores the exaggerations of conventional sentiment. And Shakespeare's treatment breaks down Phebe's stereotyped attitudes to a human reality:

he lightly suggests an adolescent perversity underlying her resistance
to love. The imagery she uses in disputing with Silvius is masterfully
squeamish, at once preoccupied with touch and shrinking from it:

> 'Tis pretty, sure, and very probable
> That eyes, which are the frail'st and softest things,
> Who shut their coward gates on atomies,
> Should be call'd tyrants, butchers, murderers!
> . . . lean but upon a rush,
> The cicatrice and capable impressure
> Thy palm some moment keeps; but now mine eyes,
> Which I have darted at thee, hurt thee not . . .

Rosalind, before whom this resistance melts, appears in her boy's
disguise "like a ripe sister," and the qualities Phebe picks out to
praise are feminine. She has, in effect, a girlish crush on the femininity
which shows through Rosalind's disguise; the aberrant affection is
happily got over when Rosalind reveals her identity and makes it
manifest that Phebe has been loving a woman. "Nature to her bias
drew in that" is the comment in *Twelfth Night* when Olivia, another
perverse girl, is fortunately extricated from a similar mistaken affection.

Touchstone's affair with Audrey complements the spectacle of exaggerated sentiment by showing love reduced to its lowest common
denominator, without any sentiment at all. The fool is detached,
objective, and resigned when the true-blue lover should be

> All made of passion, and all made of wishes,
> All adoration, duty and observance.

He explains to Jaques his reluctant reasons for getting married:

> *Jaques.* Will you be married, motley?
> *Touchstone.* As the ox hath his bow, sir, the horse his curb, and the falcon
> her bells, so man hath his desires; and as pigeons bill, so wedlock would
> be nibbling.

This reverses the relation between desire and its object, as experienced
by the four other lovers. They are first overwhelmed by the beauty of
their mistresses, then impelled by that beauty to desire them. With
Touchstone, matters go the other way about: he discovers that man
has his troublesome desires, as the horse his curb; then he decides to
cope with the situation by marrying Audrey:

> Come, sweet Audrey.
> We must be married, or we must live in bawdry.

Like all the motives which Touchstone acknowledges, this priority
of desire to attraction is degrading and humiliating. One of the hall-

marks of chivalric and Petrarchan idealism is, of course, the high valuation of the lover's mistress, the assumption that his desire springs entirely from her beauty. This attitude of the poets has contributed to that progressively increasing respect for women so fruitful in modern culture. But to assume that only one girl will do is, after all, an extreme, an ideal attitude: the other half of the truth, which lies in wait to mock sublimity, is instinct—the need of a woman, even if she be an Audrey, because "as pigeons bill, so wedlock would be nibbling." As Touchstone put it on another occasion:

> If the cat will after kind,
> So be sure will Rosalinde.

The result of including in Touchstone a representative of what in love is unromantic is not, however, to undercut the play's romance: on the contrary, the fool's cynicism, or one-sided realism, forestalls the cynicism with which the audience might greet a play where his sort of realism had been ignored. One way of describing his function is to say that he acts as a scapegoat for Arden, by taking upon himself and rendering ridiculous the side of human nature which runs counter to its perfection. We have a certain sympathy for his downright point of view, not only in connection with love but also in his acknowledgement of the vain and self-gratifying desires excluded by pastoral humility; he embodies the part of ourselves which resists the play's reigning idealism. But he does not do so in a fashion to set himself up in opposition to the play. Romantic commentators construed him as "Hamlet in motley," a devastating critic. They forgot, characteristically, that he is ridiculous: for actually he makes his attitudes preposterous when he values rank and comfort above humility, or follows biology rather than beauty. In laughing at him, we reject the tendency in ourselves which he for the moment represents: the same rejection of the primitive scapegoat was more rigorously symbolized by driving him off into the mountains. The net effect of the fool's part is thus to consolidate the hold of the serious themes by exorcising opposition. The final Shakespearean touch is to make the fool aware that in humiliating himself he is performing a public service. He goes through his part with an irony founded on the fact (and it is a fact) that he is only making manifest the folly which others, including the audience, hide from themselves.

Technically, his love affair can be called a burlesque, because throughout it there is a latent or explicit comparison with ideal lovemaking. It constitutes a comically degraded imitation. Because Shakespeare in his comedy makes fun of idealized life—not, as a satirist does, of real life—burlesque is the principal technique of his humor. His comic accompaniments consist of aberrant imitations in which the ideal norm is rendered ridiculous. We tend to think of burlesque as a generalized sort of parody, where the intention is to make fun of qualities of style, as in Fielding's *Tom Thumb*. Shakespeare's burlesque, however, imitates the ideal content of art, or indeed of artificial life, rather than artistic form. The mockery so characteristic of his comedy amounts to a kind of applied burlesque: the mocker describes his butt so as to make him out a preposterous imitation of his ideal self. A clown or fool, whose actions are accepted as burlesque, can mock merely by likening others to himself, by offering them his cap and bells. For example, Touchstone mocks the other lovers simply by referring to them as "the rest of the country copulatives." There are many ways of imitating or describing an ideal action so as to make it ridiculous. But the two principal methods can be distinguished roughly as degradation and exaggeration: the comic version either reduces the ideal to something beneath it, or carries it to an outlandish extreme. This in general is the difference between Touchstone's degraded variation on the theme of love and the exaggerated version exhibited by Silvius and Phebe.

Romantic participation in love and humorous detachment from its follies, the two polar attitudes which are balanced against each other in the action as a whole, meet and are reconciled in Rosalind's personality. Because she remains always aware of love's illusions while she herself is swept along delightfully by its deepest currents, she possesses as an attribute to character the power of combining wholehearted feeling and undistorted judgment which gives the play its value. Shakespeare exploits her situation in disguise to permit her to furnish the humorous commentary on her own ardent love affair, thus keeping comic and serious actions going at the same time. In her pretended role of saucy shepherd youth, she can mock at romance and burlesque its gestures while playing the game of putting Orlando through his paces as a suitor, to "cure" him of love. But for the audience, her disguise is transparent, and through it they see the very ardor which she mocks. When, for example, she stages a gayly overdone take-off of the conventional impatience of the lover, her own real impatience comes through the burlesque; yet the fact that she makes fun of exaggerations of the feeling conveys an awareness that it has limits, that there is a difference between romantic hyperbole and human nature:

> *Orlando.* For these two hours, Rosalind, I will leave thee.
> *Rosalind.* Alas, dear love, I cannot lack thee two hours.
> *Orlando.* I must attend the duke at dinner. By two o'clock, I will be with thee again.
> *Rosalind.* Ay, go your ways, go your ways! I knew what you would prove. My friends told me as much, and I thought no less. That flattering

tongue of yours won me. 'Tis but one cast away, and so, come death! Two o'clock is your hour?

One effect of this indirect, humorous method of conveying feeling is that Rosalind is not committed to the conventional language and attitudes of love, loaded as these inevitably are with sentimentality. Silvius and Phebe are her foils in this: they take their conventional language and their conventional feelings perfectly seriously, with nothing in reserve. As a result they seem naïve and rather trivial. They are no more than what they say, until Rosalind comes forward to realize their personalities for the audience by suggesting what they humanly are beneath what they romantically think themselves. By contrast, the heroine, in expressing her own love, conveys by her humorous tone a valuation of her sentiments, and so realizes her own personality for herself, without being indebted to another for the favor. She uses the convention where Phebe, being unaware of its exaggerations, abuses it, and Silvius, equally naïve about hyperbole, lets it abuse him. This control of tone is one of the great contributions of Shakespeare's comedy to his dramatic art as a whole. In his early plays we can see him struggling, often with indifferent success, to differentiate his characters from their sentiments by external devices of plot and situation, for example, Richard III's "hypocrisy." Later, the discipline of comedy in controlling the humorous potentialities of a remark enables the dramatist to express the relation of a speaker to his lines, including the relation of naïvete. The focus of attention is transferred from the outward action of saying something to the shifting, uncrystallized life which motivates what it said.

Without this technical resource, Rosalind could never have been created; for her peculiar charm lies less in what she does as a lover than in her attitude towards being in love. The full realization of this attitude in the great scene of disguised wooing marks the climax of the play's romantic movement. It is achieved when Rosalind is able, in the midst of her golden moment, to look beyond it and mock its illusions, including the master illusion that love is an ultimate and final experience, a matter of life and death. Ideally, love should be final, and Orlando is romantically convinced that his is so, that he would die if Rosalind refused him. But Rosalind humorously corrects him, from behind her page's disguise:

> *Rosalind.* . . . Am I not your Rosalind?
> *Orlando.* I take some joy to say you are, because I would be talking of her.
> *Rosalind.* Well, in her person, I say I will not have you.
> *Orlando.* Then, in mine own person, I die.
> *Rosalind.* No, faith, die by attorney. The poor world is almost six thousand years old, and in all this time there was not any man died in his own person, videlicet, in a love cause. Troilus had his brains dash'd out

with a Grecian club; yet he did what he could to die before, and he is
one of the patterns of love. Leander, he would have liv'd many a fair
year though Hero had turn'd nun, if it had not been for a hot midsummer night; for (good youth) he went but forth to wash him in the
Hellespont, and being taken with the cramp, was drown'd; and the
foolish chroniclers of that age found it was 'Hero of Sestos.' But these
are all lies. Men have died from time to time, and worms have eaten
them, but not for love.

Orlando. I would not have my right Rosalind of this mind, for I protest
her frown might kill me.

Rosalind. By this hand, it will not kill a fly!

A note almost of sadness comes through Rosalind's mockery towards
the end. It is not sorrow that men die from time to time, but that
they do not die for love, that love is not so final as romance would
have it. For a moment we experience as pathos the tension between
feeling and judgment which is behind all the laughter. The same
pathos of objectivity is expressed by Chaucer in the sad smile of
Pandarus as he contemplates the illusions of Troilus's love. But in
As You Like It the mood is dominant only in the moment when the
last resistance of feeling to judgment is being surmounted: the illusions
thrown up by feeling are mastered by laughter and so love is reconciled with judgment. This resolution is complete by the close of the
wooing scene. As Rosalind rides the crest of a wave of happy fulfillment (for Orlando's behavior to the pretended Rosalind has made it
perfectly plain that he loves the real one) we find her describing
with delight, almost in triumph, not the virtues of marriage, but its
fallibility:

> Say 'a day' without the 'ever.' No, no, Orlando! Men are April when
> they woo, December when they wed. Maids are May when they are maids,
> but the sky changes when they are wives.

Ordinarily, these would be strange sentiments to proclaim with joy
at such a time. But as Rosalind says them, they clinch the achievement
of the humor's purpose. Love has been made independent of illusions
without becoming any the less intense; it is therefore safe against life's
unromantic contradictions. To emphasize by humor the limitations
of the experience has become a way of asserting its reality. The scenes
which follow move rapidly and deftly to complete the consummation
of the love affairs on the level of plot. The treatment becomes more
and more frankly artificial, to end with a masque. But the lack of
realism in presentation does not matter, because a much more important realism in our attitude towards the substance of romance
has been achieved already by the action of the comedy.

In connection with Marvell and the metaphysical poets, T. S.

Eliot has made familiar an "alliance of levity and seriousness . . .
by which the seriousness is intensified." What he has said about the
contribution of wit to this poetry is strikingly applicable to the
function of Shakespeare's comedy in *As You Like It:* wit conveys
"a recognition, implicit in the expression of every experience, of
other kinds of experience which are possible." The likeness does not
consist in the fact that the wit of certain of Shakespeare's characters
at times is like the wit of Donne and his school. The real similarity
is in the way the humor functions to implement a wider awareness,
maintaining proportion where less disciplined and coherent art falsifies
by presenting a part as though it were the whole. The dramatic form
is very different from the lyric: Shakespeare does not have or need
the sustained, inclusive poise of metaphysical poetry when, at its rare
best, it fulfills Cowley's ideal:

> In a true piece of Wit all things must be
> Yet all things there agree.

The dramatist tends to show us one thing at a time, and to realize
that one thing, in its moment, to the full; his characters go to extremes, comical as well as serious; and no character, not even a
Rosalind, is in a position to see all around the play and so be completely poised, for if this were so the play would cease to be dramatic.
Shakespeare, moreover, has an Elizabethan delight in extremes for
their own sake, beyond the requirements of his form and sometimes
damaging to it, an expansiveness which was subordinated later by
the seventeenth century's conscious need for coherence. But his extremes, where his art is at its best, are balanced in the whole work.
He uses his broad-stroked, wide-swung comedy for the same end that
the seventeenth-century poets achieved by their wire-drawn wit. In
Silvius and Phebe he exhibits the ridiculous (and perverse) possibilities
of that exaggerated romanticism which the metaphysicals so often
mocked in their serious love poems. In Touchstone he includes a
representative of just those aspects of love which are not romantic,
hypostatizing as a character what in direct lyric expression would be
an irony:

> Love's not so pure and abstract as they use
> To say who have no mistress but their muse.

By Rosalind's mockery a sense of love's limitations is kept alive at
the very moments when we most feel its power:

> But at my back I always hear
> Time's wingèd chariot hurrying near.

The fundamental common characteristic is that the humor is not

directed at "some outside sentimentality or stupidity," but is an agency
for achieving proportion of judgment and feeling about a seriously
felt experience.

By no means all of Shakespeare's burlesque and mocking comedy
is as closely integrated by its function in the dramatic whole as that in
As You Like It. He often introduced such humor more or less at
random because no serious theme emerged from his material as the
object for comic commentary. *Twelfth Night* is a case in point: taken
part by part, it is as fine, or finer, than *As You Like It;* yet it is dis-
tinctly inferior as a play, because the comedy does not bear on a
central experience. The playwright, moreover, wrote a great deal of
plain and fancy farce, where the amusement springs entirely from
manipulating situations and no object for the humor is in question.
And though he never wrote social satire, for which he lacked the necessary party or class animus, he created realistic caricatures of social
types such as Doll Tearsheet and Shallow, and of humor types such
as Lucio and Parolles. But this more naturalistic comedy, magnificent
as it is, only brings into play a limited part of his genius: in creating
it he keeps one hand, so to speak, behind his back. The burlesque
and mocking humor, by contrast, can be an instrument responsive
to the full range of Shakespeare's shaping power of imagination. For
when the comedy, fulfilling its intrinsic formal possibilities as imitation, becomes a commentary on and a response to the serious heart
of a play, the play's whole meaning is involved in it. This integration
is most entire in *A Midsummer-Night's Dream, The First Part of Henry
IV, As You Like It, Hamlet, Troilus and Cressida,* and *King Lear.*
It is notable that the best humor, considered in isolation, is that which
points beyond itself.

The traditional division into Comedies, Histories and Tragedies
has obscured the way Shakespeare really put his plays together, for
his use of burlesque cuts right across these categories. He wrote only
three whole comedies: *The Comedy of Errors, The Taming of the
Shrew,* and *The Merry Wives of Windsor;* and these three pieces are
predominantly farce. Elsewhere, he always had serious matters in
hand: most of the other plays called Comedies are better described as
romances with more or less of comic accompaniment. And his practice,
once he had reached maturity, was to use comedy wherever there
was occasion for it, not simply in connection with romance. By and
large, there is more, though not better, comedy in the romances than
in plays of the other categories, because a romantic theme and a
happy ending usually called for a more extensive comic response
to strike a balance. But Shakespeare's greatest comic achievement is
in a history play with a happy ending, *Henry IV, Part I.* And when,
in the tragedies, the tragic action proper is at a standstill, as in Ham-

let's long periods of inactivity, or in the second and fourth acts of *King Lear,* the dramatist employs burlesque and mockery. For this type of comedy is an alternative method of doing what tragedy does: both forms express the difference between what life might be and what it is, and both function to adjust our feelings to the difference, the one by laughter, the other by purgative pity and fear. The final effect of both is reconciliation to reality without sentimentality or cynicism.

As You Like It[1]

by Harold Jenkins

A masterpiece is not to be explained, and to attempt to explain it is apt to seem ridiculous. I must say at once that I propose nothing so ambitious. I merely hope, by looking at one play, even in what must necessarily be a very fragmentary way and with my own imperfect sight, to illustrate something of what Shakespeare's method in comedy may be. And I have chosen *As You Like It* because it seems to me to exhibit, most clearly of all the comedies, Shakespeare's characteristic excellence in this kind. This is not to say that *As You Like It* is exactly a representative specimen. Indeed I am going to suggest that it is not. In this play, what I take to be Shakespeare's distinctive virtues as a writer of comedy have their fullest scope; but in order that they may have it, certain of the usual ingredients of Shakespeare's comedy, or indeed of any comedy, have to be—not of course eliminated, but very much circumscribed. In *As You Like It,* I suggest, Shakespeare took his comedy in one direction nearly as far as it could go. And then, as occasionally happens in Shakespeare's career, when he has developed his art far in one direction, in the comedy which succeeds he seems to readjust his course.

If our chronology is right, after *As You Like It* comes, among the comedies, *Twelfth Night.* And while we may accept that *Twelfth Night* is, as Sir Edmund Chambers says, very much akin to *As You Like It* "in style and temper," in some important respects it returns to the method and structure of the previous comedy of *Much Ado About Nothing.* Sandwiched between these two, *As You Like It* is conspicuously lacking in comedy's more robust and boisterous elements —the pomps of Dogberry and the romps of Sir Toby. More significantly, it has nothing which corresponds to the splendid theatricalism of the church scene in *Much Ado,* nothing which answers to those

[1] A lecture delivered to the Shakespeare Conference at Stratford-upon-Avon, 18 August 1953.

crucial bits of trickery by which Benedick and Beatrice in turn are hoodwinked into love. Even if, as may be objected, they are not hoodwinked but merely tricked into removing their hoods, still those stratagems in Leonato's orchard are necessary if the happy ending proper to the comedy is to be brought about. These ambushes, if I may call them so—they are really inverted ambushes—are paralleled, or should one say parodied, in *Twelfth Night* in the scene where Malvolio is persuaded that he too is beloved. And this ambush too is necessary if, as the comedy demands, Malvolio is to have his sanity called in question and his authority undermined. The slandering of Hero in *Much Ado* also is to have its counterpart in *Twelfth Night*. For the slandering of Hero, with its culmination in the church scene, forces one pair of lovers violently apart while bringing another pair together. And in *Twelfth Night* the confusion of identities holds one pair of lovers—Orsino and Viola—temporarily apart, yet forces another pair—Olivia and Sebastian—with some violence together. A satisfactory outcome in *Much Ado* and *Twelfth Night* depends on such embroilments; and the same is even more true in an earlier comedy like *A Midsummer-Night's Dream*. In *As You Like It* I can hardly say that such embroilments do not occur, but they are not structural to anything like the same degree. Without the heroine's masculine disguise Phebe would not have married Silvius any more than in *Twelfth Night* Olivia would have married Sebastian; but the confusions of identity in *As You Like It* have no influence whatever upon the ultimate destiny of Rosalind and Orlando, or of the kingdom of Duke Senior, or of the estate of Sir Rowland de Boys. Yet these are the destinies with which the action of the play is concerned. It is in the defectiveness of its action that *As You Like It* differs from the rest of the major comedies —in its dearth not only of big theatrical scenes but of events linked together by the logical intricacies of cause and effect. Of comedy, as of tragedy, action is the first essential; but *As You Like It* suggests that action is not, if I may adapt a phrase of Marston's, "the life of these things." It may be merely the foundation on which they are built. And *As You Like It* further shows that on a very flimsy foundation, if only you are skillful enough, a very elaborate structure may be poised. But the method has its dangers; and though Shakespeare's skill conceals these dangers from us, *Twelfth Night*, as I said, returns to a more orthodox scheme.

The story which provides the action for *As You Like It* belongs to the world of fairytale or folklore. This is a world which supplied the plots of a number of Shakespeare's plays, including the greatest, notably *King Lear*. And fairytales have many advantages for the dramatist, among which is their total disregard of practical probabilities. In fairytales, for example, evil is always absolute, clearly recognized, and

finally overthrown; all of which may have something to do with the
Aristotelian theory that while history records what has happened,
poetry shows what should happen. Relaxing the more prosaic demands of verisimilitude, the fairytale invites the imagination. It can
certainly provide a convenient road into the Forest of Arden. And this
is not less true for Shakespeare because the road had already been built
for him by Lodge.

A man has died and left three sons. Three is the inevitable number,
and though Shakespeare, like Lodge, forgets to do much with the
middle one, he is not therefore unimportant. The eldest brother is
wicked, the youngest virtuous—and does fabulous feats of strength,
notably destroying a giant in the shape of Charles the wrestler, who
has torn other hopeful youths to pieces. Orlando therefore wins the
princess, herself the victim of a wicked uncle, who has usurped her
father's throne. This is the *story* of *As You Like It*. And Shakespeare,
making the journey of the imagination far more quickly than Lodge,
gets most of it over in the first act. That is what is remarkable. By the
time we reach the second act Rosalind has already come safe to the
Forest of Arden, by the aid of her man's disguise. From this disguise,
as everybody knows, springs the principal comic situation of the play.
But such is the inconsequential nature of the action that this comic
situation develops only when the practical need for the disguise is
past. The course of true love has not run smooth. But most of its
obstacles have really disappeared before the main comedy begins. It
only remains for the wicked to be converted, as they duly are at the
end, all in comedy's good but arbitrary time, when the wicked eldest
brother makes a suitable husband for the second princess. Or a most
*un*suitable husband, as all the critics have complained. But this, I
think, is to misunderstand. Instead of lamenting that Celia should be
thrown away on Oliver, he having been much too wicked to deserve
her, we should rather see that Oliver's getting this reward is a seal set
on his conversion, and a sign of how good he has now become.

The first act of *As You Like It* has to supply the necessary minimum
of event. But, Quiller-Couch notwithstanding, this first act is something more than mechanical.[2] It is for one thing a feat of compression,
rapid, lucid and, incidentally, theatrical. In fifty lines we know all
about the three brothers and the youngest is at the eldest's throat. In
three hundred more we know all about the banished Duke and where
and how he lives, and the giant has been destroyed before our eyes.
But there is more to the first act than this. Before we enter Arden, to
"fleet the time carelessly, as they did in the golden world," we must be
able to contrast its simple life with the brittle refinement of the court.

[2] Quiller-Couch, *Shakespeare's Workmanship* (1918), p. 130. In spite of some
radical disagreement, I have got a number of hints from "Q" 's essay.

This surely is the point of some of what "Q" called the "rather point-less chop-logic"; and also of the courtier figure of Le Beau—a little sketch for Osric—with his foppery of diction and his expert knowledge of sport. Le Beau's notion of sport provokes Touchstone's pointed com-ment on the courtier's values: "Thus men may grow wiser every day: it is the first time that ever I heard breaking of ribs was sport for ladies." This *is* the callousness one learns at a court ruled by a tyrannous duke, whose malevolent rage against Rosalind and Orlando not only drives them both to Arden but completes the picture of the world they leave behind.

This first act, then, shows some instinct for dramatic preparation, though we may grant that Shakespeare's haste to get ahead makes him curiously perfunctory. He is in two minds about when Duke Senior was banished; and about which Duke is to be called Frederick; and whether Rosalind or Celia is the taller. He has not quite decided about the character of Touchstone. I do not think these are signs of re-vision. They simply show Shakespeare plunging into his play with some of its details still but half-shaped in his mind. The strangest of these details is the mysterious middle brother, called Fernandyne by Lodge but merely "Second Brother" in *As You Like It,* when at length he makes his appearance at the end. Yet in the fifth line of the play he was already christened Jaques. And Shakespeare of course afterwards gave this name to someone else. It seems clear enough that these two men with the same name were originally meant to be one. As things turned out Jaques could claim to have acquired his famous melancholy from travel and experience; but I suspect that it really began in the schoolbooks which were studied with such profit by Jaques de Boys. Though he grew into something very different, Jaques surely had his beginnings in the family of De Boys and in such an academy as that in Navarre where four young men turned their backs on love and life in the belief that they could supply the want of experience by study and contemplation.

Interesting as it might be to develop this idea, the important point of comparison between *As You Like It* and *Love's Labour's Lost* is of another kind. And to this I should like briefly to refer before I come to discuss the main part of *As You Like It. Love's Labour's Lost* is the one play before *As You Like It* in which Shakespeare sought to write a comedy with the minimum of action. Four young men make a vow to have nothing to do with a woman; each breaks his oath and ends vowing to serve a woman. That is the story; far slighter than in *As You Like It.* Yet, in contrast with *As You Like It,* the careful and conspicuous organization of *Love's Labour's Lost* distributes its thin action evenly through the play. And the characters always act in con-cert. In the first act the men, all together, make their vow; in the second the ladies, all together, arrive and the temptation begins. The climax duly comes, where you would expect it, in a big scene in Act IV, when each in turn breaks his vow and all together are found out. *Love's Labour's Lost* is the most formally constructed of all the comedies. When the ladies and gentlemen temporarily exchange partners, this is done symmetrically and to order. Indeed the movement of the whole play is like a well-ordered dance in which each of the participants repeats the steps of the others. But this is exactly what does *not* happen in *As You Like It*, where the characters do *not* keep in step. When they *seem* to be doing the same thing they are really doing something different, and if they ever echo one another they mean quite different things by what they say—as could easily be illustrated from the little quartet of lovers in the fifth act ("And so am I for Phebe.—And I for Ganymede.—And I for Rosalind.—And I for no woman"), where the similarity of the tune they sing conceals their different situations. The pattern of *As You Like It* comes not from a mere repetition of steps, but from constant little shifts and changes. The formal parallelisms of *Love's Labour's Lost* are replaced by a more complex design, one loose enough to hold all sorts of asymmetries within it.

But of course the effect of variations upon a theme instead of simple repetitions is not new in *As You Like It*. It is the tendency of Shakespeare's comedy from the start. In *Love's Labour's Lost* itself the courtly gestures of the four young men are burlesqued by those of a fantastic knight, and while the four young men are vowing not to see a woman, Costard the clown is "taken with a wench." Moreover, one of the four, though he goes through the movements with the others, has some trouble to keep in step, and is always threatening to break out of the ring. Even when he makes his vow with the others, he knows that necessity will make him break it. As he joins in their purposes he knows them to be foolish and he mocks at ideals which he at the same time pursues. Human activity offers itself to the dramatist in a large variety of forms and the same individual can play contradictory parts. The drunken tinker in *The Taming of the Shrew* does not know whether he may not really be a noble lord. Although Shakespeare did not invent this situation, it was just the thing to appeal to him. For he knew that a man is very easily "translated." In the middle of his fairy play he put a man with an ass's head. In perhaps the most remarkable encounter in Shakespeare the daintiest fairy queen caresses a man turned brute, who, with a fairy kingdom around him, can think only of scratching his itch. When the animal appears in a man it may terrify his fellows; it may also attract to it his finest dreams and fancies, corrupting them, or being uplifted by them to a vision of new wonder. Shakespeare of course does nothing as crude as *say* this. He knows as well as the Duke in Arden that sermons may be found in stones, but much better than the Duke that it is tedious to preach them, a thing, incidentally, he does not permit the Duke to do. What Shakespeare characteristically does in his comedy is to set together the contrasting elements in human nature and leave them by their juxtaposition or interaction to comment on one another.

In *As You Like It* the art of comic juxtaposition is at its subtlest. It is to give it fullest scope that the action can be pushed up into a corner, and the usual entanglements of plotting, though not dispensed with altogether, can be loosened. Freedom, of course, is in the hospitable air of Arden, where convenient caves stand ready to receive outlaws, alfresco meals are abundantly provided, with a concert of birds and running brooks, and there is no worse hardship than a salubrious winter wind. This is "the golden world" to which, with the beginning of his second act, Shakespeare at once transports us—such a world as has been the dream of poets since at least the time of Virgil when, wearied with the toilings and wranglings of society, they yearn for the simplicity and innocence of what they choose to think man's natural state.[3] It is of course a very literary tradition that Shakespeare is here using, but the long vogue of the pastoral suggests that it is connected with a universal impulse of the human mind, to which Shakespeare in *As You Like It* gives permanent expression. But this aspect of the play is merely the one which confronts us most conspicuously. There are many others. *As You Like It* has been too often praised for its idyllic quality alone, as though it were some mere May-morning frolic prolonged into a lotos-eating afternoon. A contrast with the ideal state was necessitated by the literary tradition itself, since the poet seeking an escape into the simple life was expected to hint at the ills of the society he was escaping from. That meant especially the courts of princes, where life—it was axiomatic—was at its most artificial. And the vivid sketching in of the courtly half of the antithesis is, as I have shown, an important function of *As You Like It*'s maligned first act. With the first speech of the banished Duke at the opening of the second act, the complete contrast is before us; for, while introducing us to Arden, this speech brings into sharp focus that first act which has just culminated in the usurper's murderous malice. "Are not these woods more free from peril than the envious court?" Though the contrast is

[3] This is not to imply that Shakespeare's "golden world" is at all the same as the primitive life of the mythical golden age, in which, by contrast with the Forest of Arden, there was no winter wind, sheep went unshorn, and man, at peace with all creatures, neither killed the deer nor was threatened by the snake and lion. Virgil associated the simplicity of pastoral life with the golden age, and the two ideals were frequently combined, not to say confused, by later pastoralists (cf. Roy Walker, *The Golden Feast* [1952], p. 133).

traditional, it comes upon us here, like so many things in Shakespeare, with the vitality of fresh experience. The Forest of Arden comes to life in numerous little touches of the country-side, and the heartless self-seeking of the outer world is concentrated into phrases which have the force of permanent truth. The line that "Q" admired—"And un-regarded age in corners thrown"—might have come from one of the sonnets; and when Orlando observes how "none will sweat but for promotion" we recognize the fashion of our times as well as his. As the play proceeds, it is easy enough for Shakespeare to keep us ever aware of the forest, what with Amiens to sing for us, the procession home after the killing of the deer, an empty cottage standing ready for Rosalind and Celia, surrounded by olive trees beyond a willow stream, and a good supply of oaks for Orlando or Oliver to lie under. It cannot have been quite so easy to keep us in touch with the court life we have now abandoned; but nothing is neater in the construction of the play than those well-placed little scenes which, by dispatching first Orlando and then Oliver to the forest, do what is still required by the story and give the illusion that an action is still going briskly forward, while at the same time they renew our acquaintance with the wicked world. After the first scene in the ideal world of Arden and a sentimental discourse on the deer, there is Frederick again in one of his rages, sending for Oliver, who, an act later, when we are well acclimatized to the forest, duly turns up at court. Then occurs a scene of eighteen lines, in which Shakespeare gives as vivid a sketch of the unjust tyrant as one could hope to find. The tyrant prides himself upon his mercy, punishes one man for his brother's sins, and finds in his victim's excuses further cause of offense. Oliver's plaint that he had never loved his brother brings the instant retort, "More villain thou. Well, push him out of doors." As this eruption dies down, there appears in the Forest of Arden the cause of all the trouble quietly hanging his verses on a tree.

The contrast between court and country is thus presented and our preference is very plain. Yet as a counterpoise to all this, there is one man in the countryside who actually prefers the court. Finding him-self in Arden, Touchstone decides: "When I was at home, I was in a better place." It is no doubt important that he is a fool, whose values may well be topsy-turvy. But in one word he reminds us that there are such things as domestic comforts. And presently we find that the old man whom society throws into the corner is likely in the "uncouth forest" to die of hunger and exposure to the "bleak air." There is clearly something to be said on the other side; the fool may anatomize the wise man's folly. And there is also Jaques to point out that the natural life in Arden, where men usurp the forest from the deer and kill them in their "native dwelling-place," while deer, like men, are

in distress abandoned by their friends, is as cruel and unnatural as
the other. When Amiens sings under the greenwood tree and turns "his
merry note unto the sweet bird's throat," inviting us to shun ambition
and be pleased with what we get, Jaques adds a further stanza to the
song which suggests that to leave your "wealth and ease" is the act of an
ass or a fool. Most of us, I suppose, have moods in which we would
certainly agree with him; and it is a mark of Shakespeare's mature
comedy that he permits this criticism of his ideal world in the very
center of it. The triumphal procession after the killing of the deer,
a symbolic ritual of the forester's prowess, is accompanied by a mocking song, while the slayer of the deer is given its horns to wear as a
somewhat ambiguous trophy.

It is Jaques, mostly, with the touch of the medieval buffoon in him,
who contributes this grotesque element to the songs and rituals of
Arden. Like Touchstone he is not impressed by Arden; but unlike
Touchstone he does not prefer the court. Indeed, as we have seen, he is
able to show that they are very much alike, infected by the same
diseases. No doubt his is a jaundiced view of life; and it is strange that
some earlier critics should have thought it might be Shakespeare's.
Shakespeare's contemporaries would hardly have had difficulty in
recognizing in Jaques a variant of the Elizabethan melancholy man—
the epithet is applied to him often enough—though I remain a little
sceptical when I am told by O. J. Campbell that from the first moment they heard Jaques described, the Elizabethans would have
perceived "the unnatural melancholy produced by the adustion of
phlegm." [4] Whatever its physiological kind, the important thing about
his melancholy is that it is not the fatigue of spirits of the man who has
found the world too much for him, but an active principle manifesting
itself in tireless and exuberant antics. Far from being a morose man,
whether he is weeping with the stag or jeering at the huntsman, he
throws himself into these things with something akin to passion. His
misanthropy is a form of self-indulgence, as is plain enough in his very
first words:

> *Jaques.* More, more, I prithee, more.
> *Amiens.* It will make you melancholy, Monsieur Jaques.
> *Jaques.* I thank it. More, I prithee, more. I can suck melancholy out of
> a song.

His own comparison with a weasel sucking eggs suggests what a fero-
cious and life-destroying thing this passion is. Shakespeare's final dis-
missal of Jaques is profound. Far from making Celia a better husband
than Oliver, as George Sand apparently thought, he is the one person

[4] *Huntington Library Bulletin,* VIII (1935), 85.

in the play who could not be allowed to marry anyone, since he can have nothing to do with either love or generation. His attempt to forward the nuptials of Touchstone and Audrey serves only to postpone them. He is of course the one consistent character in the play in that he declines to go back with the others to the court that they have scorned. Yet how *can* he go back when the court has been converted? Jaques's occupation's gone. And he will not easily thrive away from the social life on which he feeds. It is notable that the place he really covets, or affects to, is that of the motley fool, licensed to mock at society, indulged by society but not of it. Yet, seeking for a fool, he has only to look in the brook to find one; and it is the romantic hero who will tell him so.

Shakespeare, then, builds up his ideal world and lets his idealists scorn the real one. But into their midst he introduces people who mock their ideals and others who mock *them.* One must not say that Shakespeare never judges, but one judgment is always being modified by another. Opposite views may contradict one another, but of course they do not cancel out. Instead they add up to an all-embracing view far larger and more satisfying than any one of them in itself.

Now when Orlando tells Jaques that he may see a fool by looking in the brook, this is not the first time that Jaques and Orlando meet; and the relations between the two of them are worth a moment's glance. Their first encounter occurs in public when the Duke and his retinue are met for one of their forest repasts. Jaques has just been eloquent about the vices of mankind and is justifying the satirist who scourges them, when he is confronted with the romantic hero in his most heroic attitude, rushing into the middle of the scene with drawn sword,[5] crying, "Forbear, and eat no more." But Jaques is not the man to be discomposed, even when a sudden interruption throws him off his hobby-horse. When he has inquired, "Of what kind should this cock come of?", the heroic attitude begins to look extravagant. The hero stands his ground: "Forbear, I say: He dies that touches any of this fruit"; at which Jaques nonchalantly helps himself to a grape, saying, "An you will not be answered with reason (raisin), I must die." Heroism now appears thoroughly deflated, or would do if Jaques were attended to by the company at large. The hero is in fact saved by the Duke's "civility"; and their talk of "gentleness" and "nurture" even throws back into perspective Jaques's recent attack upon society. The situation as a whole retains its equilibrium. And yet as a result of this little incident we are bound to feel that the romantic hero is very vulnerable to the ridicule of the satirist, until their duel of wit in the following act readjusts our view by allowing Orlando his retort.

[5] *"Enter Orlando"* says the Folio simply, but the dialogue justifies Theobald's *"with Sword drawn."*

There is a formal point to notice here, easy to miss but full of meaning. The wit-combat between Jaques and the hero is matched an act or
so later—there is no strict regularity about these things—by a similar
wit-combat between Jaques and the heroine. On each occasion Jaques
is worsted and departs, leaving Rosalind and Orlando to come together. In fact the discomfiture of Monsieur Melancholy by one or
other of the lovers is the prelude to each of the two big love scenes of
the play. And this arrangement makes a point more prettily than any
action-plot involving Jaques could do. The mocking words of Jaques's
farewell are in each case illuminating: "Farewell, good Signior Love";
and "Nay, then, God be wi' you, an you talk in blank verse." The gibe
at blank verse is not an incidental or decorative jest. It makes it clear
that, however we judge of them, the melancholy spirit of Jaques and
the romantic emotion of Rosalind and Orlando cannot mingle. Shakespeare dismisses the melancholy man before he gives the lovers their
scope. And in this I follow his example.

So far I have dealt only with the immigrants to Arden. There is
of course a native population. The natural world of the poet's dreams
has always been inhabited by shepherds, who from the time of Theoc-
ritus have piped their songs of love. And Rosalind and Celia have
been in the forest for only twenty lines when two shepherds appear
pat before them. In an earlier comedy perhaps these might have been
a similar pair singing comparable love ditties. But in *As You Like It*
—Shakespeare making the most of what is offered him by Lodge—they
are a contrasting pair. One is young and one is old, one is in love and
one is not. The lover is the standard type. But the notion of love has
undergone a change since classical times and the shepherds of Renaissance pastorals have all been bred in the schools of courtly love. So
young Silvius is the faithful abject lover who finds disdain in his fair
shepherdess's eye and sighs "upon a midnight pillow"—Shakespeare
always fixes on a detail in which a whole situation is epitomized. There
are of course many other lovers in the play, but the story of Silvius
and Phebe is of the pure pastoral world, the familiar literary norm
against which all the others may be measured. First against Silvius and
Phebe are set Rosalind and Orlando, and the immediate result of this
is that Rosalind and Orlando, though they clearly belong to the
pastoral world, seem much closer to the ordinary one. Indeed, since
Silvius and Phebe relieve them of the necessity of displaying the lovers'
more extravagant postures, Rosalind and Orlando are freer to act like
human beings. Rosalind need only play at taunting her adorer while
allowing her real woman's heart to be in love with him in earnest. In
an earlier comedy like *The Two Gentlemen of Verona* the heroes themselves had to undergo those "bitter fasts, with penitential groans, With
nightly tears and daily heart-sore sighs," and these are what, as H. B.

Charlton says, may make Valentine look a fool. But with Silvius to take this burden from him, Orlando can really be a hero, performing the traditional hero's fabulous feats, and upon occasion may even be a common man like ourselves. He has, for example, the very human trait of unpunctuality; he is twice late for an appointment. And although on one occasion he has the perfect excuse of a bloody accident, on the other he has nothing to say, beyond "My fair Rosalind, I come within an hour of my promise." Such engaging casualness is of course outside Silvius's range. And although Orlando has his due share of lovers' sighs and is indeed the "unfortunate he" who hangs the verses on the trees, in so human a creature these love-gestures appear not as his *raison d'être* but as an aberration. A delightful aberration, no doubt—"I would not be cured, youth," he says—but still an aberration that can be the legitimate subject of our mockery. Lying contemplating his love under an oak, he seems to Celia "like a dropped acorn," and both the ladies smile at his youthful lack of beard. But Orlando is robust enough to stand their mockery and ours, and Shakespeare's superb dramatic tact arranges that Orlando shall draw our laughter towards him so that he may protect the fragile Silvius from the ridicule which would destroy *him*. Rosalind alone is privileged to make fun of Silvius; and that because searching his wounds, she finds her own. The encounters which do not occur have their significance as well as those which do: Touchstone is only once, and Jaques never, allowed a sight of Silvius before the final scene of the play. Silvius has not to be destroyed or the play will lack something near its center.

If in a pastoral play the ideal shepherd is satirized it must be indirectly. But that he is, through his complete unreality, a likely target for satire has been commonly recognized by the poets, who have therefore had a habit of providing him with a burlesque counterpart to redress the balance and show that they did know what rustics were like in real life. As Gay was to put it in his proem to *The Shepherd's Week,* the shepherd "sleepeth not under myrtle shades, but under a hedge"; and so when Gay's shepherd makes love it is in a sly kiss behind a haycock to the accompaniment of the lady's yells of laughter. This may have been the method of Shakespeare's William, for, far from inditing verses to his mistress, William is singularly tongue-tied; though he is "five and twenty" and thinks he has "a pretty wit," the biggest of his eleven speeches is only seven words long. And his partner is just as much a contrast to the shepherdess of pastoral legend. She thanks the gods she is not beautiful, does not even know the meaning of "poetical," and her sheep, alas, are goats.

Shakespeare, then, presents the conventional pastoral, and duly burlesques it. But with surer knowledge of life than many poets have had, he seems to suspect that the burlesque as well as the convention may also miss the truth. Do shepherds really sleep under hedges? In order to be unsophisticated, must they be stupid too? So among his varied array of shepherds, Silvius and Ganymede and William, Shakespeare introduces yet another shepherd, the only one who knows anything of sheep, whose hands even get greasy with handling them. It does not matter that Shakespeare got the hint for Corin from Corydon in Lodge. For Lodge found Corydon in literature and for Corin Shakespeare went to life. Lodge's Corydon, though he may make the king smile with his clownish salutation, has evidently been bred at court himself. Would he ever else accost a lady in distress in strains like these

> If I should not, fair damosel, occasion offence, or renew your griefs by rubbing the scar, I would fain crave so much favour as to know the cause of your misfortunes.

Shakespeare's Corin speaks at once of grazing and shearing and an unkind master; and when he talks about the shepherd's life he shows that he knows the value of money and that fat sheep need good pasture. His greatest pride is to see his ewes graze and his lambs suck. This is the note of his philosophy, and if it has its limitations, it is far from despicable and is splendidly anchored to fact. His attitude to love is that of the fully sane man undisturbed by illusions. Being a man, he has been in love and can still guess what it is like; but it is so long ago he has forgotten all the details. How little he belongs to Arcadia may be discovered from Sidney, whose shepherd-boy went on piping "as though he should never be old." In *As You Like It* perpetual youth is the happiness of Silvius, and his fate. *That* much of the difference between Silvius and Corin is apparent from the short dialogue of twenty lines which first introduces them together to us.

In Corin Shakespeare provides us with a touchstone with which to test the pastoral. Corin's dialogue with the Touchstone of the court, dropped into the middle of the play, adds to the conventional anti-thesis between courtier and countryman a glimpse of the real thing. Our picture of the court as a place of tyranny, ambition and corruption is no doubt true enough. But its colors are modified somewhat when Touchstone gives us the court's plain routine. For him, as he lets us know on another occasion, the court is the place where he has trod a measure, flattered a lady, been smooth with his enemy and undone three tailors. Though Touchstone seeks to entangle Corin in the fantastications of his wit, his arguments to show that the court is better than the sheepfarm have a way of recoiling on himself. What emerges from the encounter of these two realists is

that ewe and ram, like man and woman, are put together and that
though the courtier perfumes his body it sweats like any other
creature's. In city or country, *all* ways of life are at bottom the same,
and we recognize a conclusion that Jaques, by a different route, has
helped us to reach before.

The melancholy moralizings of Jaques and the Robin Hood raptures
of the Duke, though in contrast, are equally the product of man's
spirit. There has to be someone in Arden to remind us of the indispensable flesh. It was a shrewd irony of Shakespeare's to give this
office to the jester. Whether he is wiser or more foolish than other
men, it is never possible to decide, but Touchstone is, as well as
the most artificial wit, the most natural man of them all; and the
most conscious of his corporal needs. After the journey to the forest
Rosalind complains of a weariness of spirits, to which Touchstone
retorts "I care not for my spirits, if my legs were not weary." And
when he displays his wit at the expense of Orlando's bad verses,
saying "I'll rhyme you so eight years together," he remembers to
add "dinners and suppers and sleeping-hours excepted." A "material
fool," as Jaques notes. This preoccupation with the physical makes
Touchstone the obvious choice for the sensual lover who will burlesque
the romantic dream. So Touchstone not only deprives the yokel
William of his mistress, but steals his part in the play, making it
in the process of infinitely greater significance. However, Shakespeare
from the beginning cast Touchstone for this burlesque role, though
he may not have seen at first what form the burlesque would take.
When Silvius first exhibits his love to us, and reminds Rosalind of
hers, Touchstone completes the trio on his discordant note:

> I remember, when I was in love I broke my sword upon a stone and
> bid him take that for coming a-night to Jane Smile; and I remember
> the kissing of . . . the cow's dugs that her pretty chopt hands had
> milked.

This sort of extravagance—in the burlesque-chivalrous vein—is not, I
think, developed; but an indecent jest about a peascod does point
forward to the animal lust which propels him towards Audrey, and
his amour with her forms the perfect contrast to the three idealized
courtships of the play. If we need a formal juxtaposition of the two
kinds of love to point the matter further, I note that it is just when
Rosalind has met Orlando in the forest and Orlando has promised
to woo her "by the faith of [his] love" and "with all [his] heart" that
we see Touchstone courting the goat-girl, regretting that fair women
should be honest and talking of sexual desire.

The fool is not only a material touchstone; he is also the timekeeper of the play. At least, in the forest, where "there's no clock,"

he carries a time-piece with him; and it provokes the reflection: "It is ten o'clock . . . 'Tis but an hour ago since it was nine, And after one hour more 'twill be eleven." The people of Arcadia will do well to take note of this, but if all you can do with your hours is to count them, this undeniable truth may seem a trifle futile. Touchstone, to do him justice, goes on: "And so, from hour to hour, we ripe and ripe, And then, from hour to hour, we rot and rot." He dares to speak in Arcadia, where one can never grow old, of Time's inevitable processes of maturity and decay. By this the ideal life of the banished Duke is mocked, and since Touchstone's words are repeated by Jaques with delighted and uproarious laughter, the mockery is double. Yet, in accordance with the play's principle of countering one view with another, there are two things that may be noted: first, that in a later scene Touchstone, who sums up life as riping and rotting, is compared by Rosalind to a medlar, which is rotten before it is ripe; and second, that it is at this very point, when the ideal life is doubly mocked, that the Duke administers to the mocker Jaques a direct and fierce rebuke, charging the mocker of the world's vices with having lived a vicious life himself.

The satirist, of course, is far from silenced; it is now that he ridicules the romantic hero, and presently he delivers his famous speech on the seven ages of man, brilliantly summing up the course of human life, but omitting to notice anything in it that is noble or even pleasant. However, as has often been observed, though the seven ages speech ends with a description of man's final decrepitude— "sans teeth, sans eyes, sans taste, sans everything"—it has not yet left the speaker's tongue when an aged man appears who is at once addressed as "venerable." There is always this readjustment of the point of view. Senility and venerableness—are they different things or different ways of looking at the same? Certainly the entry of the venerable Adam does not disprove what Jaques says; Shakespeare seeks no cheap antithesis. "Sans teeth"—Adam himself has admitted to being toothless, Orlando has called him a "rotten tree," and his help-lessness is only too visible when he is *carried* on to the stage. Yet he *is* carried, tenderly, by the master whom he has followed "to the last gasp, with truth and loyalty." Here is the glimpse of human virtue that the seven ages speech omitted. And then it is upon this moving spectacle of mutual affection and devotion that Amiens sings his song, "Blow, blow, thou winter wind, Thou art not so unkind As man's ingratitude." Placed here, this lovely lyric, blend of joy and pathos, has a special poignancy.

The arrangement of the play depends upon many such piquant but seemingly casual juxtapositions. *As You Like It* contemplates life within and without Arden, with numerous shifts of angle, alternating valuations of mood. As for action, incident—life in the Forest of Arden does not easily lend itself to those. I have suggested that Shakespeare does something to supply this want by a glance or two back at what is happening at court. And departures from the court are matched by arrivals in the forest. For events, of course, even in Arden do sometimes occur. Orlando arrives dramatically, even melodramatically. Presently Rosalind learns that he is about. A little later on they meet. Later still Oliver arrives and is rescued from a lioness. Shakespeare still keeps up a sense of things going on. But the manner of the play, when once it settles down in the forest, is to let two people drift together, talk a little, and part, to be followed by two more. Sometimes a pair will be watched by others, who will sometimes comment on what they see. Sometimes of course there is a larger group, once or twice even a crowded stage; but most often two at a time. When they part they may arrange to meet again, or they may not. Through the middle acts of the play, though there are two instances of love at first sight (one of them only reported), it is rare that anything happens in any particular encounter between these people of the sort that changes the course of their lives, anything, that is to say, that goes to make what is usually called a plot. Yet the meetings may properly be called "encounters," because of the impact the contrasting characters make on one another and the sparkle of wit they kindle in one another. What is important in each meeting is our impression of those who meet and of their different attitudes to one another's views of life, an impression which is deepened or modified each time they reappear with the same or different partners. As I describe it, this may all sound rather static, but such is the ease and rapidity with which pairs and groups break up, re-form, and succeed one another on the stage that there is a sense of fluid movement. All is done with the utmost lightness and gaiety, but as the lovers move through the forest, part and meet again, or mingle with the other characters in their constantly changing pairs and groups, every view of life that is presented seems, sooner or later, to find its opposite. Life is "but a flower in spring time, the only pretty ring time," but for the unromantic Touchstone there is "no great matter in the ditty" and he counts it but time lost—his eye no doubt still on his timepiece—"to hear such a foolish song." A quartet of lovers avowing their love is broken up when one of them says

> Pray you, no more of this; 'tis like the howling of Irish wolves against the moon.

And the one who says this is she who cannot tell "how many fathom deep" she is in love. Dominating the center of the play, playing both the man's and woman's parts, counselor in love and yet its victim,

Rosalind gathers up into herself many of its roles and many of its meanings. Around her in the forest, where the banished Duke presides, is the perfect happiness of the simple life, an illusion, much mocked at, but still cherished. She herself, beloved of the hero, has all the sanity to recognize that "love is merely a madness" and that lovers should be whipped as madmen are, but admits that "the whippers are in love too." Heroine of numerous masquerades, she is nonetheless always constant and never more true than when insisting that she is counterfeiting. For she is an expert in those dark riddles which mean exactly what they say. Though things are rarely what they seem, they may sometimes be so in a deeper sense. What is wisdom and what is folly is of course never decided—you may have it "as you like it." Or, as Touchstone rejoined to Rosalind, after her gibe about the medlar, "You have said; but whether wisely or no, let the forest judge."

It may be possible to suggest that the forest gives its verdict. For if *As You Like It* proclaims no final truth, its ultimate effect is not negative. Longing to escape to our enchanted world, we are constantly brought up against reality; sanity, practical wisdom sees through our illusions. Yet in *As You Like It* ideals, though always on the point of dissolving, are forever recreating themselves. They do not delude the eye of reason, yet faith in them is not extinguished in spite of all that reason can do. "I would not be cured, youth."

Planes of Reality[1]

by S. L. Bethell

There is no need to summarize what is known of the structure and physical conditions of the Elizabethan theatre, since this has been well done by a number of writers. It is necessary, however, to stress certain relevant factors.[2] As galleries ran all round the theater, even above the back of the stage, the actors could be seen from every direction, as in a circus. Below them, in the roofless yard, groundlings crowded close on three sides of the projecting apron; whilst even more embarrassing was the proximity of those young men of fashion who, hiring stools upon the stage itself, displayed their own rich costume in competition with the company's wardrobe. Even with the abundance of makeup, scenery, and properties in use today, it would have been impossible for actors so closely beset with audience, to create and sustain an illusion of actual life, especially as they performed in broad daylight. In Shakespeare's time painted scenery was, in fact, used hardly at all; and as the "act drop" was still unknown, stools, benches, and other properties must have been carried on and off in full sight of the audience; beds, we know, were directed to be "thrust out" on to the stage, complete with occupant. A small set might be prepared on the "inner stage" behind a drawn curtain; but this was possible only for scenes of small dimension, such as the Capulets' tomb, or Belarius's cave in *Cymbeline*. In these circumstances, much of the "business" was necessarily conventional: a siege was represented by an attack upon the tiring house, with scaling ladders erected against the gallery above. There was some crude realism, and a scene of violent death might be

---

"Planes of Reality." From Shakespeare and the Popular Dramatic Tradition *by* S. L. Bethell *(London: P. S. King and Staples, Ltd., 1944), Chapter Two, pp. 31-41. Copyright 1944 by P. S. King and Staples, Ltd. Reprinted by permission of Mrs. M. R. Bethell.*

[1] I have taken this term, and with it a valuable suggestion, from *Shakespeare's Last Plays*, by E. M. W. Tillyard (Chatto & Windus, 1938).
[2] My facts are taken from E. K. Chambers: *The Elizabethan Stage*, 4 vols. (Clarendon Press, 1923), from *Shakespeare and the Theatre*, and from the works of Miss M. C. Bradbrook [*Elizabethan Stage Conditions* (Cambridge, 1932) and *Themes and Conventions of Elizabethan Tragedy* (Cambridge, 1935)].

44

rendered more convincing by pricking a bladder of vinegar (presumably beneath the victim's shirt), as is directed in the pre-Shakespearean *Cambises*: Shakespeare himself seems to have discarded such obvious methods after his early experimental plays. The sort of realism represented by a fully furnished drawing room set in Ibsen or Pinero was, of course, unattainable, and seems hardly to have been desired. The Elizabethans relied on their poetry for much that is nowadays left to the producer. Though more subtly efficient than our modern stage mechanism in securing the appropriate responses, the use of verse marks in itself a further remove from naturalism. Verse goes with conventionalism, whilst naturalism logically implies a colloquial prose. This accounts for the inappropriateness of Victorian productions of Shakespeare, where naturalistic settings conflicted with the subtler atmospheric suggestions of the verse.

The inability of the Elizabethan theater to produce an illusion of actuality was wholly to the good, as modern experimental theaters have shown. At a standard presentation of Ibsen, the audience remain passively receptive; whilst in another, two-dimensional world, beyond the orchestra pit, within a picture frame and behind footlights, the actors create a vivid illusion of actual life. In the Elizabethan, or the modern experimental theater, there is no illusion of actual life; but the audience are vividly aware of acting in progress, and the communication, through their cooperative goodwill, of a work of dramatic art. If the one type of production is more realistic, the other is essentially more real.

Shakespeare, despite an occasional grumble at the inadequacy of his "wooden O" (*Henry V*, Prol. 13), wisely accepted the situation as it was, and turned it to good. Perhaps he would have welcomed the resources at Ibsen's command, but fortunately he was safe from temptation. I do not suggest that he had any conscious insight into the advantages of his own position; indeed, its strength lay partly in the unconscious acceptance, by both playwright and audience, of conditions as they found them. But Shakespeare did not merely acquiesce in those limitations which the physical conditions of his theater placed upon dramatic illusion; he actually exploited them, so that conventions in production are integrally related to conventions in the treatment of history, in the presentation of character, and in the verse. Moreover, he even draws attention to the play as play, overtly, in the dialogue itself, emphasizing verbally what the manner of production already implied: the coexistence of play-world and real world in the minds of his audience. Perhaps when characters within a play referred to plays and players, or noted that "All the world's a stage" (*As You Like It*, II. vii. 139), a certain piquancy in the situation may have been all that forced itself into conscious attention. As they had never experienced naturalistic drama, the Elizabethans would not appreciate, as we do today, the nature of their own drama in distinction from it— just as it is impossible to appreciate a state of physical well-being until suffering has supplied us with a standard of comparison. But this double consciousness of play-world and real world has the solid advantage of distancing a play, so that the words and deeds of which it consists may be critically weighed in the course of its performance. An Ibsen drama, attended to passively, is discussed afterwards in abstract terms; but in a Shakespearean play, criticism is an integral part of apprehension, and apprehension thereby becomes an activity of the whole mind. This is, of course, due mainly to the fact that the verse must be understood for a proper appreciation of the action; but the detachment necessary for attention to the verse is gained by insisting on the essential artificiality of the play-world, and thus holding play-world and real world before the mind simultaneously yet without confusion. Such an attitude has the advantage of accepting and exploiting the situation as it really is, whereas naturalism must engage in a constant effort to delude the audience into taking for actuality what they are bound to know, in their moments of critical alertness, to be only a stage performance. To gain a hearing, naturalism destroys the critical awareness necessary for appreciation: it is hardly surprising that a method thus divided against itself has produced little of permanent value.

When Malvolio appears before Olivia's household, cross-gartered and in "the trick of singularity" (*Twelfth Night*, II. v. 164), Signor Fabian has an interesting comment:

> If this were played upon a stage now, I could condemn it as an improbable fiction.

> (III. iv. 140)

It is, of course, an improbable fiction, and Shakespeare is employing a common enough literary device to cope with it. There are a great many novelists whose characters exclaim: "Why, it's just like a novel!" This sort of remark carries more than one layer of suggestion. Superficially it makes an improbable situation more plausible. If the characters displayed no consciousness of its improbability we should be left with a rankling doubt; but since they react as we do to the situation, we are able to accept its improbability, and incorporate it into the world of fiction. At the same time, whatever illusion may have been created has now been broken through: Shakespeare's mention of "playing upon a stage" forcibly reminds his audience of the nature of the spectacle before them. A naturalistic writer plays with fire when he attempts this sort of thing; but in the Elizabethan theater, with an audience continually aware of the two worlds of fiction and reality side by side, the effect is at the same time to justify an improbable situation, and to underline the essential unreality of the play-world. This latter function is much the more important: Shakespeare was not sufficiently concerned for probability and consistency to have inserted Fabian's comment merely for the sake of verisimilitude. It occurs at a significant juncture, when the baiting of Malvolio is about to be carried to extremes. The passage continues:

> *Sir Toby.* His very genius hath taken the infection of the device, man.
> *Maria.* Nay, pursue him now, lest the device take air and taint.
> *Fabian.* Why, we shall make him mad indeed.
> *Maria.* The house will be the quieter.
> *Sir Toby.* Come, we'll have him in a dark room and bound. . . .
>
> (III. iv. 142)

The Victorians, who sympathized with Malvolio's sufferings to the extent of creating him a tragic hero, and who disdained the Elizabethan crudity which could enjoy Sir Toby's horseplay, failed to perceive that the Elizabethans were not in the habit of mistaking their comedies for real life. Shakespeare erected, through Fabian, a plain enough notice for his audience, and for the Victorians too, if they had taken trouble over his text. We are reminded that the play is only a play, just when the reminder is needed to enable us to enjoy the comedy of Malvolio's imprisonment. The original audience would take such a hint unconsciously, but the Victorians, cut off from the popular tradition, preferred to discover the tragedy which Shakespeare was so careful not to write.

This explanation of Shakespeare's deeper—and surely unconscious —intention may seem far-fetched, and would never have occurred to me had I considered only the passage from *Twelfth Night*. But elsewhere there are similar reminders of the play as play, without any ostensible design of rendering plausible an improbable incident. Indeed, in *Love's Labour's Lost*, the immediate intention is diametrically opposite: to excuse a naturalistic departure from the normal theatrical habit of ending a light comedy with wedding bells. *Love's Labour's Lost* is the most artificial of Shakespeare's comedies; the only note of ungarbled seriousness occurs at the end, when Biron is condemned to "jest a twelvemonth in an hospital" (*Love's Labour's Lost*, V. ii. 881), as a cure for levity and a preliminary to marriage. The unusual task imposed by Rosaline upon her knight breaks incongruously into the abstract gaiety of a simplified play-world, bearing a sharp reminder of suffering and sorrow, ingredients of the real world hitherto unheeded through five acts of artificial wit-combat. This bitter reminder of the real world is underlined and at the same time distanced by the ensuing remarks of Biron and the king:

Biron. Our wooing doth not end like an old play;
　　Jack hath not Jill: these ladies' courtesy
　　Might well have made our sport a comedy.
King. Come, sir, it wants a twelvemonth and a day,
　　And then 'twill end.
Biron.　　　　　　　　That's too long for a play.

(V. ii. 884)

The young Shakespeare, commenting in public on his technique, reinforces the dual consciousness of play-world and real world in the
minds of his audience. A play so artificial may end quite appropriately
with a reference from within to its own true nature. But, coming immediately after the hospital theme, this passage serves a more delicate
purpose. With its reminder of reality, as distinguished from the play-
world, it underlines the reference to human suffering by taking us
back to the real world where it is to be encountered. At the same
time, by making explicit the nature of the play as play, it preserves a
threatened poise: we remember that it is a stage personage only who
is to "jest a twelvemonth in an hospital," and that personal sympathy
would be misplaced. The intellectual position of the comedy has been
strengthened, whilst its "artificiality" has been satisfactorily restored.

In plot and setting, *As You Like It* is every whit as artificial as *Love's
Labour's Lost.* There is the same movement of lovers in patterned
pairs (with two temporary triangles as an added complication in the
later play); and the masque of Hymen completes a general, if superficial, resemblance to the modern "musical comedy." The dialogue is
easy and relatively mature: Rosalind's prose in the Forest of Arden is
so natural-seeming that as a character she "comes alive" mainly by
this means; but Shakespeare is the more careful to provide a balance
of artificiality in his verse, and to indicate through his verse-technique
the varying degrees of actuality to which we are expected to adjust
ourselves. This explains the antiphonal echoing of phrases between
Orlando and Duke Senior, when the former bursts in upon the exiles
with his demand for hospitality:

Orlando. . . . .
　　If ever you have look'd on better days,
　　If ever been where bells have knoll'd to church,
　　If ever sat at any good man's feast,
　　If ever from your eyelids wiped a tear
　　And know what 'tis to pity and be pitied,
　　. . . .
Duke Senior. True is it that we have seen better days,
　　And have with holy bell been knoll'd to church
　　And sat at good men's feasts and wiped our eyes

Of drops that sacred pity hath engender'd:

. . . .

                    (*As You Like It*, II. vii. 113)

This careful pattern of question and answer distances and tones down
a scene where otherwise emotion might run too high. The tendency
throughout is to pass lightly over whatever has the potentiality of
heightened emotion, in order, presumably, to keep the intellect un-
clouded and to concentrate serious attention upon certain themes:
court *versus* country, literary pastoral and the clod-hopping rustic,
tradition and innovation in rural economy. And so the love-tangle
resolves itself at a level of actuality similar to the average Gilbert and
Sullivan opera. The lovers' repetitive phrases have the effect of "Three
little maids from school":

> *Silvius*. It is to be all made of sighs and tears;
>   And so am I for Phebe.
> *Phebe*. And I for Ganymede.
> *Orlando*. And I for Rosalind.
> *Rosalind*. And I for no woman.
>
>   (V. ii. 90)

In the next scene, the lovers pair off appropriately, and Rosalind is
reunited to her father mostly in rhyme and as an integral part of the
masque of Hymen.

Apart from such obvious instances in which verse-technique is used
to distance the dramatic experience, it would be possible to grade all
the verse in an ascending scale of artificiality, from the broken, vigor-
ous dialogue of Duke Frederick, to the near-burlesque of Silvius and
Phebe. Duke Frederick has the sort of verse which develops in the
tragedies:

> She is too subtle for thee; and her smoothness,
> Her very silence and her patience
> Speak to the people, and they pity her.
> Thou art a fool: she robs thee of thy name;
> And thou wilt show more bright and seem more virtuous
> When she is gone. Then open not thy lips:
> Firm and irrevocable is my doom
> Which I have passed upon her; she is banish'd.
>
>   (I. iii. 79)

Contrast:

> *Silvius*. Sweet Phebe, do not scorn me; do not, Phebe;
>   Say that you love me not, but say not so

In bitterness. The common executioner,
Whose heart the accustom'd sight of death makes hard,
Falls not the axe upon the humbled neck
But first begs pardon: will you sterner be
Than he that dies and lives by bloody drops?

(III. v. i.)

This is rhythmically more regular; the fourth and sixth lines have
the pointless inversions of a strained "poetic" style; and the conceit
has a certain obvious ingenuity typically Petrarchan. Between the extremes that I have quoted lies a wide range of delicately perceptible
differences in style, all indicating degrees of remoteness from actuality.
At this time Shakespeare seems to have been serious in prose—there
is more prose than verse in *As You Like It*—and to have used verse
mainly to emphasize the conventional. This view of the matter is
borne out in a significant remark of Jaques. Orlando enters and ad-
dresses Rosalind, who, as Ganymede, has been effectively ridiculing
Jaques' melancholy:

Orlando. Good day and happiness, dear Rosalind!
Jaques. Nay, then, God be wi' you, and you talk in blank verse.

(IV. i. 30)

The incident is, I suppose, explicable in naturalistic terms: Orlando
utters an involuntary blank verse line, and the cynical Jaques seizes
upon it to make his escape with an implied sneer against the lover.
But, in any event, the mention of blank verse by a character draws
attention to the play as play, in the same way as the remarks of Fabian
and Biron, already discussed. Jaques' Parthian shot goes farther, however, by associating blank verse with the conventions of fashionable
wooing, and thus suggesting that the play's artificiality is especially
constituted by the verse. We have seen that this is, in fact, true of *As
You Like It*.

Deliberate emphasis upon the unreality of the play-world is uncom-
mon nowadays. It is still, however, an habitual device of the Marx
brothers, those excellent Hollywood comedians, who combine the wild-
est nonsense with a delicate satirical probing of the defective values
in our modern civilization. Their methods are purely conventional,
and they require above everything an alert audience, ready to grasp
at every word and each significant gesture. It would be fatal for their
purpose if the audience were to become emotionally involved in the
thin line of romantic story which holds their performance together.
In their best film, *Animal Crackers*, which appeared some years ago,
there are two direct reminders of the film as film. Groucho forgets the
name of the character he represents, and turning to the audience, demands a program: this is complicated by the reference back from film

to "legitimate" stage, since programs are not provided in the cinema. At another point in the film, he reminds us after a feeble pun, that "You can't expect all the jokes to be good." I do not know whether the Marx brothers are consciously aware, any more than Shakespeare is likely to have been, that this type of joke has an important effect upon the relationship of actors and audience. They have continued to employ it in more recent films with remarkable consistency, and this indicates at least a strong instinctive sense of its usefulness. In *The Marx Brothers Go West* we were told as (I think) the engine driver was being gagged: "This is the best gag in the picture"; and in *The Big Store,* when the villain is finally unmasked, Groucho exclaims, echoing the average comment from the stalls: "I could have told you in the first reel he was a crook." The effect is the same as in Shakespeare: it reinforces the double consciousness of play-world and real world and at the same time it distances the play as play, and produces intimacy with the audience for the actor as actor rather than as character.

It has already been observed that the acting of female parts by boys was further complicated by the frequency with which the story demanded a male disguise. It is usually said that the boy would welcome relief for a time from the embarrassment of his unaccustomed garments, and would probably act the better for being unencumbered. Since the investigation of Elizabethan theatrical conditions opened a new field of conjecture, "practical" explanations of this kind have been carried to excess. A boy would soon learn to manage his skirts without thinking of them—girls do, and the talent is unlikely to be inherited. It is better to seek explanations in the nature of Shakespeare's sources, and in the psychology of an audience to which the principle of multiconsciousness applies. Probably the situation of "boy playing girl playing boy" pleased in its suggestion of multiple planes of reality. It would, of course, be a pleasure entirely dependent upon the dual consciousness of play-world and real world. I have seen, at a concert-party performance, a female impersonator (i.e., a man who habitually plays women's parts) playing the part of a woman in man's clothes. A popular audience clearly recognized and enjoyed the unusual situation. Cleopatra's objection to a Roman triumph:

> . . . I shall see
> Some squeaking Cleopatra boy my greatness
> I' the posture of a whore,
>
> (*Antony and Cleopatra,* V. ii. 219)

effects through dialogue a precisely similar complication in the planes of reality. Also, as a direct reference to acting, it performs the same function as the other passages I have considered, bringing forcibly to mind the duality of play-world and real world. This passage is especially remarkable since it occurs in a tragedy and at a moment of great emotional intensity. Moreover, *Antony and Cleopatra* comes at the end of the tragic period, when Shakespeare has learnt all there is to learn about his art. An alert and critically detached audience is implied, and an attitude to tragedy very different from that to which we are accustomed.

Children are always fascinated by the notion of infinite regression. I remember a certain biscuit tin which always gave me, as a small boy, a distinct sense of the "numinous." It had on it a picture of a boy holding a tin just like the real one, and on the tin the boy held was another picture of a boy holding a tin. The childish question, "And who made God?" betrays a similar interest. The concern of Shakespeare and the Elizabethans with "planes of reality," shows, not, of course, their childishness, but a healthy preoccupation with the questions men naturally ask when undeterred by the advances of civilization. The "play-within-the-play," as in *A Midsummer-Night's Dream* and *Hamlet,* or the device by which the main play is presented before a stage audience, as in *The Taming of the Shrew* or Kyd's *Spanish Tragedy,* further illustrates the same preoccupation. An audience watches a stage audience watching a play, and so becomes simultaneously aware of three planes of reality. Shakespeare carries the matter farther by his frequent metaphorical use of play and players. To Jaques "All the world's a stage . . ." (*As You Like It,* II. vii. 139), and to Macbeth

> Life's but a walking shadow, a poor player
> That struts and frets his hour upon the stage
> And then is heard no more.
>
> (*Macbeth,* V. v. 24)

Contemplation of regression, which produced the parlor games of Viola-Cesario and Hamlet's Mousetrap, has here assumed philosophical significance. The solidity of the first plane of reality, the plane of our terrestrial life, is seen to be illusory. It is significant that in the last fully Shakespearean play, the planes of reality appear with most complexity. Prospero says of his Masque of Ceres:

> These our actors,
> As I foretold you, were all spirits and
> Are melted into air, into thin air.
>
> (*The Tempest,* IV. i. 148)

"On the actual stage," observes Dr. Tillyard, "the masque is executed by players pretending to be spirits, pretending to be real actors, pretending to be supposed goddesses and rustics." [3] And immediately after the revels end, Prospero reminds us that, as his spirit actors have vanished, so

> The cloud-capped towers, the gorgeous palaces,
> The solemn temples, the great globe itself,
> Yea, all which it inherit, shall dissolve
> And, like this insubstantial pageant faded,
> Leave not a rack behind. We are such stuff
> As dreams are made on, and our little life
> Is rounded with a sleep.
>
> (IV. i. 152)

The world is seen as transient, and therefore insubstantial, whilst a reference to the dream world adds a further complication. It seems as if Shakespeare had deliberately crowded into a few moments of his last play all that can suggest the manifold mystery of experience. Both Jaques and Macbeth employed the play metaphor to express an attitude of cynicism: in Jaques, the cynicism which was a recognized ingredient of contemporary fashionable melancholy; in Macbeth, the cynicism of a hardened sinner, who, having rejected the laws of God and man, cut off from all sympathetic contact with the world outside himself, has become incapable of apprehending meaning in that world. But Prospero's speech begins:

> You do look, my son, in a moved sort,
> As if you were dismay'd: be cheerful, sir.
>
> (IV. i. 146)

To Prospero, whose "beating mind" (IV. i. 163) achieves at this moment an insight into reality, the transitoriness of this world is matter for cheerfulness. We are therefore justified in pushing the parallel farther, and remembering that, though the actors have faded, as invisible spirits they still exist; and that from sleep there is awakening. Sleep, in Shakespeare, is always regarded as remedial:

> Sleep that knits up the ravell'd sleave of care,
> The death of each day's life, sore labour's bath,
> Balm of hurt minds, great nature's second course,
> Chief nourisher in life's feast. . . .
>
> (*Macbeth*, II. ii. 37)

If, as seems likely, Prospero in his great speech voices Shakespeare's own conclusions, then this passage, far from proclaiming the agnosti-

---

[3] *Shakespeare's Last Plays*, p. 80.

cism of a world-weary artist, clearly asserts, at the culmination of a life-long and unique poetic experience, the existence of an eternal order behind the relatively trivial and impermanent phenomenal world, as the "real" world exists in comparative stability behind the shadow world of the theater. The survival of human persons after their sleep of death is incidentally implied. The final organization of Shakespeare's experience is thus functionally related to the dual consciousness of play-world and real world, characteristic of Elizabethan playhouse psychology. If Shakespeare put the whole of life into his plays, he reciprocally interpreted life in terms of the theater.

As You Like It

by Helen Gardner

As its title declares, this is a play to please all tastes. It is the last play in the world to be solemn over; and there is more than a touch of absurdity in delivering a lecture, particularly on a lovely summer morning, on this radiant blend of fantasy, romance, wit and humor. The play itself provides its own ironic comment on anyone who attempts to speak about it: You have said; but whether wisely or no, let the forest judge.

For the simple, it provides the stock ingredients of romance: a handsome, well-mannered young hero, the youngest of three brothers, two disguised princesses to be wooed and wed, and a banished, virtuous duke to be restored to his rightful throne. For the more sophisticated, it propounds, in the manner of the old courtly literary form of the *débat*, a question which is left to us to answer: Is it better to live in the court or the country? "How like you this shepherd's life, Master Touchstone?", asks Corin, and receives a fool's answer: "Truly, shepherd, in respect of itself, it is a good life; but in respect that it is a shepherd's life, it is naught. In respect that it is solitary, I like it very well; but in respect that it is private, it is a very vile life." Whose society would you prefer, Le Beau's or Audrey's? Would you rather be gossiped at in the court or gawped at in the country? The play has also the age-old appeal of the pastoral, and in different forms. The pastoral romance of princesses playing at being a shepherd boy and his sister is combined with the pastoral love-eclogue in the wooing of Phebe, with the burlesque of this in the wooing of Audrey, and with the tradition of the moral eclogue, in which the shepherd is the wise man, in Corin. For the learned and literary this is one of Shakespeare's most allusive plays, uniting old traditions and playing with them lightly. Then there are the songs—the forest is full of music—and there is spectacle: a wrestling match to delight lovers of sport, the

"As You Like It," by *Helen Gardner. From* More Talking of Shakespeare, *ed. John Garrett (London: Longmans, Green & Company, Ltd., 1959; New York: Theatre Arts Books, 1959), pp. 17-32. Copyright © 1959 by Longmans, Green & Company, Ltd. Reprinted by permission of Longmans, Green & Company, Ltd. and Theatre Arts Books.*

procession with the deer, which goes back to old country rituals and folk plays, and finally the masque of Hymen, to end the whole with courtly grace and dignity. This is an image of civility and true society, for Hymen is a god of cities, as Milton knew:

> There let *Hymen* oft appear
> In Saffron robe, with Taper clear,
> And pomp, and feast, and revelry,
> With mask, and antique Pageantry.

The only thing the play may be said to lack, when compared with Shakespeare's other comedies, is broad humor, the humor of gross clowns. William makes only a brief appearance. The absence of clowning may be due to an historic reason, the loss of Kempe, the company's funny man. But if this was the original reason for the absence of pure clowning, Shakespeare has turned necessity to glorious gain and made a play in which cruder humors would be out of place. *As You Like It* is the most refined and exquisite of the comedies, the one which is most consistently played over by a delighted intelligence. It is Shakespeare's most Mozartian comedy.

The basic story is a folk-tale. The ultimate sources for the plots of Shakespeare's greatest tragedy and his most unflawed comedy are stories of the same kind. The tale of the old king who had three daughters, of whom the elder two were wicked and the youngest was good, belongs to the same primitive world of the imagination as the tale of the knight who had three sons, the eldest of whom was wicked and robbed the youngest, who was gallant and good, of his inheritance. The youngest son triumphed, like Jack the Giant Killer, over a strong man, a wrestler, joined a band of outlaws in the forest, became their king, and with the aid of an old servant of his father, the wily Adam Spencer, in the end had his revenge on his brother and got his rights. Lodge retained some traces of the boisterous elements of this old story; but Shakespeare omitted them. His Orlando is no bully, threatening and blustering and breaking down the doors to feast with his boon companions in his brother's house. He is brave enough and quick tempered; but he is above all gentle. On this simple story Lodge grafted a pastoral romance in his *Rosalynde*. He made the leader of the outlaws a banished duke, and gave both exiled duke and tyrant usurper only daughters, as fast friends as their fathers are sworn enemies. The wrestling match takes place at the tyrant's court and is followed by the banishment of Rosalynde and the flight of the two girls to the forest, disguised as shepherd and shepherdess. There the shepherd boy is wooed by the gallant hero, and arouses a passion of love-sickness in a shepherdess who scorns her faithful lover. The re-

pentance of the wicked brother and his flight to the forest provide the
necessary partner for the tyrant's good daughter, and all ends happily
with marriages and the restoration of the good duke. Shakespeare
added virtually nothing to the plot of Lodge's novel. There is no
comedy in which, in one sense, he invents so little. He made the two
dukes into brothers. Just as in *King Lear* he put together two stories
of good and unkind children, so here he gives us two examples of a
brother's unkindness. This adds to the fairytale flavor of the plot,
because it turns the usurping duke into a wicked uncle. But if he invents no incidents, he leaves out a good deal. Besides omitting the
blusterings of Rosader (Orlando), he leaves out a final battle and the
death in battle of the usurping duke, preferring to have him converted
off-stage by a chance meeting with a convenient and persuasive hermit.
In the same way he handles very cursorily the repentance of the wicked
brother and his good fortune in love. In Lodge's story, the villain is
cast into prison by the tyrant who covets his estates. In prison he
repents, and it is as a penitent that he arrives in the forest. Shakespeare
also omits the incident of the attack on Ganymede and Aliena by
robbers, in which Rosader is overpowered and wounded and Saladyne
(Oliver) comes to the rescue and drives off the assailants. As has often
been pointed out, this is both a proof of the genuineness of his repentance and a reason, which many critics of the play have felt the
want of, for Celia's falling in love. Maidens naturally fall in love with
brave young men who rescue them. But Shakespeare needs to find no
"reasons for loving" in this play in which a dead shepherd's saw is
quoted as a word of truth: Whoever lov'd that lov'd not at first sight.
He has far too much other business in hand at the center and heart of
his play to find time for mere exciting incidents. He stripped Lodge's
plot down to the bare bones, using it as a kind of frame, and created
no subplot of his own. But he added four characters. Jaques, the phi-
losopher, bears the same name as the middle son of Sir Rowland de
Boys—the one whom Oliver kept at his books—who does not appear
in the play until he turns up casually at the end as a messenger. It
seems possible that the melancholy Jaques began as this middle son
and that his melancholy was in origin a scholar's melancholy. If so,
the character changed as it developed, and by the time that Shakespeare had fully conceived his cynical spectator he must have realized
that he could not be kin to Oliver and Orlando. The born solitary
must have no family: Jaques seems the quintessential only child. To
balance Jaques, as another kind of commentator, we are given Touchstone, critic and parodist of love and lovers and of court and courtiers.
And, to make up the full consort of pairs to be mated, Shakespeare
invented two rustic lovers, William and Audrey, dumb yokel and

sluttish goat-girl. These additional characters add nothing at all to the story—if you were to tell it, you would leave them out. They show us that story was not Shakespeare's concern in this play; its soul is not to be looked for there. If you were to go to *As You Like It* for the story you would, in Johnson's phrase, "hang yourself."

In an essay called "The Basis of Shakespearian Comedy" [1] Professor Nevill Coghill attempted to "establish certain things concerning the nature of comic form, as it was understood at Shakespeare's time." He pointed out that there were two conceptions of comedy current in the sixteenth century, both going back to grammarians of the fourth century, but radically opposed to each other. By the one definition a comedy was a story beginning in sadness and ending in happiness. By the other, it was, in Sidney's words, "an imitation of the common errors of our life" represented "in the most ridiculous and scornefull sort that may be; so that it is impossible that any beholder can be content to be such a one." Shakespeare, he declared, accepted the first; Jonson, the second. But although *As You Like It*, like *A Midsummer-Night's Dream*, certainly begins in sadness and ends with happiness, I do not feel, when we have said this, that we have gone very far towards defining the play's nature; and I do not think that the plot in either of these two lovely plays, or in the enchanting early comedy *Love's Labour's Lost*, which indeed has hardly any plot at all, can be regarded as the "soul" or animating force of Shakespeare's most original and characteristic comedies. Professor Coghill's formula fits plays which we feel rather uneasy about, *The Merchant of Venice* and *Measure for Measure*. It is precisely the stress on the plot which makes us think of these as being more properly described as tragicomedies than comedies. Neither of them is a play which we would choose as a norm of Shakespeare's genius in comedy. In *As You Like It* the plot is handled in the most perfunctory way. Shakespeare crams his first act with incident in order to get everyone to the forest as soon as he possibly can and, when he is ready, he ends it all as quickly as possible. A few lines dispose of Duke Frederick, and leave the road back to his throne empty for Duke Senior. As for the other victim of a wicked brother, it is far more important that Orlando should marry Rosalind than that he should be restored to his rights.

Mrs. Suzanne Langer, in her brilliant and suggestive book *Feeling and Form*,[2] has called comedy an image of life triumphing over chance. She declares that the essence of comedy is that it embodies in symbolic form our sense of happiness in feeling that we can meet and master

[1] *Essays and Studies* (English Association: John Murray, 1950). Reprinted in part below (View Points), p. 107.
[2] Routledge & Kegan Paul, Ltd., 1953.

the changes and chances of life as it confronts us. This seems to me to provide a good description of what we mean by "pure comedy," as distinct from the corrective or satirical comedy of Jonson. The great symbol of pure comedy is marriage by which the world is renewed; and its endings are always instinct with a sense of fresh beginnings. Its rhythm is the rhythm of the life of mankind, which goes on and re-news itself as the life of nature does. The rhythm of tragedy, on the other hand, is the rhythm of the individual life which comes to a close, and its great symbol is death. The one inescapable fact about every human being is that he must die. No skill in living, no sense of life, no inborn grace or acquired wisdom can avert this individual doom. A tragedy, which is played out under the shadow of an inevitable end, is an image of the life pattern of every one of us. A comedy, which contrives an end which is not implicit in its beginning, and which is, in itself, a fresh beginning, is an image of the flow of human life. The young wed, so that they may become in turn the older generation, whose children will wed, and so on, as long as the world lasts. Comedy pictures what Rosalind calls "the full stream of the world." At the close of a tragedy we look back over a course which has been run: The rest is silence. The end of a comedy declares that life goes on: Here we are all over again. Tragic plots must have a logic which leads to an inescapable conclusion. Comic plots are made up of changes, chances and surprises. Coincidences can destroy tragic feeling: they heighten comic feeling. It is absurd to complain in poetic comedy of improbable encounters and characters arriving pat on their cue, of sudden changes of mind and mood by which an enemy becomes a friend. Puck, who creates and presides over the central comedy of *A Midsummer-Night's Dream,* speaks for all comic writers and lovers of true comedy when he says:

> And those things do best please me
> That befall preposterously.

This aspect of life, as continually changing and presenting fresh opportunities for happiness and laughter, poetic comedy idealizes and presents to us by means of fantasy. Fantasy is the natural instrument of comedy, in which plot, which is the "soul" of tragedy, is of second-ary importance, an excuse for something else. After viewing a tragedy we have an "acquist of true experience" from a "great event." There are no "events" in comedy; there are only "happenings." Events are irreversible and comedy is not concerned with the irreversible, which is why it must always shun the presentation of death. In adapting Lodge's story Shakespeare did not allow Charles the wrestler to kill the Franklin's sons. Although they are expected to die, we may hope they will recover from their broken ribs. And he rejected also Lodge's ending in which the wicked duke was killed in battle, preferring his improbable conversion by a hermit. But why should we complain of its improbability? It is only in tragedy that second chances are not given. Comedy is full of purposes mistook, not "falling on the inventor's head" but luckily misfiring altogether. In comedy, as often happens in life, people are mercifully saved from being as wicked as they meant to be.

Generalization about the essential distinctions between tragedy and comedy is called in question, when we turn to Shakespeare, by the inclusiveness of his vision of life. In the great majority of his plays the elements are mixed. But just as he wrote one masterpiece which is purely tragic, dominated by the conception of Fate, in *Macbeth,* so he wrote some plays which embody a purely comic vision. Within the general formula that "a comedy is a play with a happy ending," which can, of course, include tragicomedies, he wrote some plays in which the story is a mere frame and the essence of the play lies in the presentation of an image of human life, not as an arena for heroic endeavor but as a place of encounters.

Tragedy is presided over by time, which urges the hero onwards to fulfill his destiny. In Shakespeare's comedies time goes by fits and starts. It is not so much a movement onwards as a space in which to work things out: a midsummer night, a space too short for us to feel time's movement, or the unmeasured time of *As You Like It* or *Twelfth Night.* The comedies are dominated by a sense of place rather than of time. In Shakespeare's earliest comedy it is not a very romantic place: the city of Ephesus. Still, it is a place where two pairs of twins are accidentally reunited, and their old father, in danger of death at the beginning, is united to his long-lost wife at the close. The substance of the play is the comic plot of mistakings, played out in a single place on a single day. The tragicomic story of original loss and final restoration provides a frame. In what is probably his second comedy, *The Two Gentlemen of Verona,* Shakespeare tried a quite different method. The play is a dramatization of a *novella;* and it contains no comic place of encounters where time seems to stand still. The story begins in Verona, passes to Milan, and ends in a forest between the two cities. None of these places exerts any hold upon our imaginations. The story simply moves forward through them. In *Love's Labour's Lost,* by contrast, Shakespeare went as far as possible in the other direction. The whole play is a kind of ballet of lovers and fantastics, danced out in the King of Navarre's park. Nearby is a village where Holofernes is the schoolmaster, Nathaniel the curate, and Dull the constable. In this play we are given, as a foil to the lords and ladies, not comic servants, parasitic on their masters, but a little comic world, society in miniature, going about its daily business while the lovers are engaged in the discovery of theirs. Shakespeare dispensed with the tragicomic frame altogether here. There is no sorrow at the beginning, only youthful male fatuity; and the "putting right" at the close lies in the chastening of the lords by the ladies. The picture of the course of life as it appears to the comic vision, with young men falling in love and young women testing their suitors, and other men "labouring in their vocations" to keep the world turning and to impress their fellows, is the whole matter of the play. Much more magical than the sunlit park of the King of Navarre is the wood near Athens where Puck plays the part of chance. Shakespeare reverted here to the structural pattern of his earliest comedy, beginning with the cruel fury of Egeus against his daughter, the rivalry of Lysander and Demetrius and the unhappiness of the scorned Helena, and ending with Theseus's overriding of the father's will and the proper pairing of the four lovers. But here he not only set his comic plot of mistakings within a frame of sorrow turning to joy, he also set his comic place of encounters apart from the real world, the palace where the play begins and ends. All the center of the play takes place in the moonlit wood where lovers immortal and mortal quarrel, change partners, are blinded, and have their eyes purged.

Having created a masterpiece, Shakespeare, who never repeated a success, went back in his next play to tragicomedy, allowing the threat of terrible disaster to grow through the play up to a great dramatic fourth act. *The Merchant of Venice* has what *The Two Gentlemen of Verona* lacks, an enchanted place. Belmont, where Bassanio goes to find his bride, and where Lorenzo flees with Jessica, and from which Portia descends like a goddess to solve the troubles of Venice, is a place apart, "above the smoke and stir." But it is not, like the wood near Athens, a place where the changes and chances of our mortal life are seen mirrored. It stands too sharply over against Venice, a place of refuge rather than a place of discovery. *Much Ado About Nothing* reverts to the single place of *The Comedy of Errors* and *Love's Labour's Lost*; and its tragicomic plot, which also comes to a climax in a dramatic scene in the fourth act, is lightened not by a shift of scene but by its interweaving with a brilliant comic plot, and by all kinds of indications that all will soon be well again. The trouble comes in the middle of this play: at the beginning, as at the end, all is revelry and happiness. A sense of holiday, of time off from the world's business, reigns in Messina. The wars are over, peace has broken out, and Don Pedro and the gentlemen have returned to where the ladies are waiting for them to take up again the game of love and wit. In the

atmosphere created by the first act, Don John's malice is a cloud no
bigger than a man's hand. And although it grows as the play proceeds,
the crisis of the fourth act is like a heavy summer thunder shower
which darkens the sky for a time but will, we know, soon pass. The
brilliant lively city of Messina is a true place of mistakings and discoveries, like the park of the King of Navarre; but, also like the park
of the King of Navarre, it lacks enchantment. It is too near the ordinary world to seem more than a partial image of human life. In
As You Like It Shakespeare returned to the pattern of *A Midsummer-
Night's Dream,* beginning his play in sorrow and ending it with joy,
and making his place of comic encounters a place set apart from the
ordinary world.

The Forest of Arden ranks with the wood near Athens and Prospero's
island as a place set apart, even though, unlike them, it is not ruled
by magic. It is set over against the envious court ruled by a tyrant,
and a home which is no home because it harbors hatred, not love.
Seen from the court it appears untouched by the discontents of life,
a place where "they fleet the time carelessly, as they did in the golden
age," the gay greenwood of Robin Hood. But, of course, it is no such
Elysium. It contains some unamiable characters. Corin's master is
churlish and Sir Oliver Martext is hardly sweet-natured; William is a
dolt and Audrey graceless. Its weather, too, is by no means always
sunny. It has a bitter winter. To Orlando, famished with hunger and
supporting the fainting Adam, it is "an uncouth forest" and a desert
where the air is bleak. He is astonished to find civility among men who

> in this desert inaccessible,
> Under the shade of melancholy boughs,
> Lose and neglect the creeping hours of time.

In fact Arden does not seem very attractive at first sight to the weary
escapers from the tyranny of the world. Rosalind's "Well, this is the
forest of Arden" does not suggest any very great enthusiasm; and to
Touchstone's "Ay, now I am in Arden; the more fool I: when I was
at home, I was in a better place: but travellers must be content," she
can only reply, "Ay, be so, good Touchstone." It is as if they all have
to wake up after a good night's rest to find what a pleasant place they
have come to. Arden is not a place for the young only. Silvius, forever
young and forever loving, is balanced by Corin, the old shepherd, who
reminds us of that other "penalty of Adam" beside "the seasons' difference": that man must labor to get himself food and clothing. Still, the
labor is pleasant and a source of pride: "I am a true labourer: I earn
that I eat, get that I wear, owe no man hate, envy no man's happiness,
glad of other men's good, content with my harm; and the greatest of

my pride is to see my ewes graze and my lambs suck." Arden is not a place where the laws of nature are abrogated and roses are without their thorns. If, in the world, Duke Frederick has usurped on Duke Senior, Duke Senior is aware that he has in his turn usurped upon the deer, the native burghers of the forest. If man does not slay and kill man, he kills the poor beasts. Life preys on life. Jaques, who can suck melancholy out of anything, points to the callousness that runs through nature itself as a mirror of the callousness of man. The herd abandons the wounded deer, as prosperous citizens pass with disdain the poor bankrupt, the failure. The race is to the swift. But this is Jaques's view. Orlando, demanding help for Adam, finds another image from nature:

> Then but forbear your food a little while,
> Whiles, like a doe, I go to find my fawn
> And give it food. There is a poor old man,
> Who after me hath many a weary step
> Limp'd in pure love: till he be first suffic'd,
> Oppress'd with two weak evils, age and hunger,
> I will not touch a bit.

The fact that they are both derived ultimately from folk-tale is not the only thing that relates *As You Like It* to *King Lear*. Adam's somber line, "And unregarded age in corners thrown," which Quiller-Couch said might have come out of one of the greater sonnets, sums up the fate of Lear:

> Dear daughter, I confess that I am old;
> Age is unnecessary: on my knees I beg
> That you'll vouchsafe me raiment, bed, and food.

At times Arden seems a place where the same bitter lessons can be learnt as Lear has to learn in his place of exile, the blasted heath. Corin's natural philosophy, which includes the knowledge that "the property of rain is to wet," is something which Lear has painfully to acquire:

> When the rain came to wet me once and the wind to make me chatter,
> when the thunder would not peace at my bidding, there I found 'em,
> there I smelt 'em out. Go to, they are not men o' their words: they told
> me I was everything; 'tis a lie, I am not ague-proof.

He is echoing Duke Senior, who smiles at the "icy fang and churlish chiding of the winter's wind," saying:

> This is no flattery: these are counsellors
> That feelingly persuade me what I am.

Amiens's lovely melancholy song:

> Blow, blow, thou winter wind,
> Thou are not so unkind
>   As man's ingratitude. . . .
>
> Freeze, freeze, thou bitter sky,
> That dost not bite so nigh
>   As benefits forgot. . . ,

is terribly echoed in Lear's outburst:

> Blow, winds, and crack your cheeks! rage! blow!
> .   .   .   .
> Rumble thy bellyful! Spit, fire! spout, rain!
> Nor rain, wind, thunder, fire, are my daughters:
> I tax not you, you elements, with unkindness;
> I never gave you kingdom, call'd you children. . . .

And Jaques's reflection that "All the world's a stage" becomes in Lear's mouth a cry of anguish:

> When we are born, we cry that we are come
> To this great stage of fools.

It is in Arden that Jaques presents his joyless picture of human life, passing from futility to futility and culminating in the nothingness of senility—"sans everything"; and in Arden also a bitter judgment on human relations is lightly passed in the twice repeated "Most friendship is feigning, most loving mere folly." But then one must add that hard on the heels of Jaques's melancholy conclusion Orlando enters with Adam in his arms, who, although he may be "sans teeth" and at the end of his usefulness as a servant, has, besides his store of virtue and his peace of conscience, the love of his master. And the play is full of signal instances of persons who do not forget benefits: Adam, Celia, Touchstone—not to mention the lords who chose to leave the court and follow their banished master to the forest. In a recent number of the *Shakespeare Survey* Professor Harold Jenkins[3] has pointed out how points of view put forward by one character find contradiction or correction by another, so that the whole play is a balance of sweet against sour, of the cynical against the idealistic, and life is shown as a mingling of hard fortune and good hap. The lords who have "turned ass," "leaving their wealth and ease a stubborn will to please," are happy in their gross folly, as Orlando is in a love-sickness which he does not wish to be cured of. What Jaques has left out of his picture of man's strange eventful

[3] In his essay reprinted above.

pilgrimage is love and companionship, sweet society, the banquet under the boughs to which Duke Senior welcomes Orlando and Adam. Although life in Arden is not wholly idyllic, and this place set apart from the world is yet touched by the world's sorrows and can be mocked at by the wordly wise, the image of life which the forest presents is irradiated by the conviction that the gay and the gentle can endure the rubs of fortune and that this earth is a place where men can find happiness in themselves and in others.

The forest of Arden is, as has often been pointed out, a place which all the exiles from the court, except one, are only too ready to leave at the close. As, when the short midsummer night is over, the lovers emerge from the wood, in their right minds and correctly paired, and return to the palace of Theseus; and, when Prospero's magic has worked the cure, the enchanted island is left to Caliban and Ariel, and its human visitors return to Naples and Milan; so the time of holiday comes to an end in Arden. The stately masque of Hymen marks the end of this interlude in the greenwood, and announces the return to a court purged of envy and baseness. Like other comic places, Arden is a place of discovery where the truth becomes clear and where each man finds himself and his true way. This discovery of truth in comedy is made through errors and mistakings. The trial and error by which we come to knowledge of ourselves and of our world is symbolized by the disguisings which are a recurrent element in all comedy, but are particularly common in Shakespeare's. Things have, as it were, to become worse before they become better, more confused and farther from the proper pattern. By misunderstandings men come to understand; and by lies and feignings they discover truth. If Rosalind, the princess, had attempted to "cure" her lover Orlando, she might have succeeded. As Ganymede, playing Rosalind, she can try him to the limit in perfect safety, and discover that she cannot mock or flout him out of his "mad humour of love to a living humour of madness," and drive him "to forswear the full stream of the world, and to live in a nook merely monastic." By playing with him in the disguise of a boy, she discovers when she can play no more. By love of a shadow, the mere image of a charming youth, Phebe discovers that it is better to love than to be loved and scorn one's lover. This discovery of truth by feigning, and of what is wisdom and what folly by debate, is the center of *As You Like It*. It is a play of meetings and encounters, of conversations and sets of wit: Orlando versus Jaques, Touchstone versus Corin, Rosalind versus Jaques, Rosalind versus Phebe, and above all Rosalind versus Orlando. The truth discovered is, at one level, a very "earthy truth": Benedick's discovery that "the world must be peopled." The honest toil of Corin,

the wise man of the forest, is mocked at by Touchstone as "simple sin."
He brings "the ewes and the rams together" and gets his living "by the
copulation of cattle." The goddess Fortune seems similarly occupied
in this play: "As the ox hath his bow, the horse his curb, and the falcon
her bells, so man hath his desires; and as pigeons bill, so wedlock
would be nibbling." Fortune acts the role of a kindly bawd. Touchstone's marriage to Audrey is a mere coupling. Rosalind's advice to
Phebe is brutally frank: "Sell when you can, you are not for all
markets." The words she uses to describe Oliver and Celia "in the very
wrath of love" are hardly delicate; and after her first meeting with
Orlando she confesses to her cousin that her sighs are for her "child's
father." Against the natural background of the life of the forest
there can be no pretense that the love of men and women can
"forget the He and She."

But Rosalind's behavior is at variance with her bold words. Orlando
has to prove that he truly is, as he seems at first sight, the right husband for her, and show himself gentle, courteous, generous, and brave,
and a match for her in wit, though a poor poet. In this, the great
coupling of the play, there is a marriage of true minds. The other
couplings run the gamut downwards from it, until we reach Touchstone's image of "a she-lamb of a twelvemonth" and "a crooked-pated,
old, cuckoldy ram," right at the bottom of the scale. As for the debate
as to where happiness is to be found, the conclusion come to is again,
like all wisdom, not very startling or original: that "minds innocent
and quiet" can find happiness in court or country:

> Happy is your Grace,
> That can translate the stubbornness of fortune
> Into so quiet and so sweet a style.

And, on the contrary, those who wish to can "suck melancholy" out of
anything, "as a weasel sucks eggs."

In the pairing one figure is left out. "I am for other than for
dancing measures," says Jaques. Leaving the hateful sight of revelling
and pastime, he betakes himself to the duke's abandoned cave, on his
way to the house of penitents where Duke Frederick has gone. The
two commentators of the play are nicely contrasted. Touchstone is the
parodist, Jaques the cynic. The parodist must love what he parodies.
We know this from literary parody. All the best parodies are written
by those who understand, because they love, the thing they mock.
Only poets who love and revere the epic can write mock-heroic and
the finest parody of classical tragedy comes from Housman, a great
scholar. In everything that Touchstone says and does gusto, high
spirits, and a zest for life ring out. Essentially comic, he can adapt himself to any situation in which he may find himself. Never at a loss, he

is life's master. The essence of clowning is adaptability and im-
provisation. The clown is never baffled and is marked by his ability to
place himself at once *en rapport* with his audience, to be all things to
all men, to perform the part which is required at the moment. Touchstone sustains many different roles. After hearing Silvius's lament and
Rosalind's echo of it, he becomes the maudlin lover of Jane Smile;
with the simple shepherd Corin he becomes the cynical and worldly
wise man of the court; with Jaques he is a melancholy moralist, musing
on the power of time and the decay of all things; with the pages he
acts the lordly amateur of the arts, patronizing his musicians. It is
right that he should parody the rest of the cast, and join the procession
into Noah's ark with his Audrey. Jaques is his opposite. He is the cynic,
the person who prefers the pleasures of superiority, cold-eyed and
cold-hearted. The tyrannical Duke Frederick and the cruel Oliver can
be converted; but not Jaques. He likes himself as he is. He does not
wish to plunge into the stream, but prefers to stand on the bank
and "fish for fancies as they pass." Sir Thomas Elyot said that dancing
was an image of matrimony: "In every daunse, of a most auncient
custome, there daunseth together a man and a woman, holding eche
other by the hande or the arme, which betokeneth concorde." There
are some who will not dance, however much they are piped to, any
more than they will weep when there is mourning. "In this theatre
of man's life," wrote Bacon, "it is reserved only for God and angels
to be lookers on." Jaques arrogates to himself the divine role. He has
opted out from the human condition.

It is characteristic of Shakespeare's comedies to include an element
that is irreconcilable, which strikes a lightly discordant note, casts a
slight shadow, and by its presence questions the completeness of the
comic vision of life. In *Love's Labour's Lost* he dared to allow the news
of a death to cloud the scene of revels at the close; and, through
Rosalind's rebuke to Berowne, called up the image of a whole world
of pain and weary suffering where "Mirth cannot move a soul in
agony." In the two comedies whose main action is motivated by hatred
and with malice thwarted but not removed, *The Merchant of Venice*
and *Much Ado About Nothing,* Shakespeare asks us to accept the fact
that the human race includes not only a good many fools and rogues
but also some persons who are positively wicked, a fact which comedy
usually ignores. They are prevented from doing the harm they wish
to do. They are not cured of wishing to do harm. Shylock's baffled
exit and Don John's flight to Messina leave the stage clear for lovers
and well-wishers. The villains have to be left out of the party at the
close. At the end of *Twelfth Night* the person who is left out is present.
The impotent misery and fury of the humiliated Malvolio's last
words, "I'll be reveng'd on the whole pack of you," call in question

the whole comic scheme by which, through misunderstandings and mistakes, people come to terms with themselves and their fellows. There are some who cannot be "taught a lesson." In Malvolio pride is not purged; it is fatally wounded and embittered. It is characteristic of the delicacy of temper of *As You Like It* that its solitary figure, its outsider, Jaques, does nothing whatever to harm anyone, and is perfectly satisfied with himself and happy in his melancholy. Even more, his melancholy is a source of pleasure and amusement to others. The duke treats him as virtually a court entertainer; and he is a natural butt for Orlando and Rosalind. Anyone in the play can put him down and feel the better for doing so. All the same, his presence casts a faint shadow. His criticism of the world has its sting drawn very early by the duke's rebuke to him as a former libertine, discharging his filth upon the world, and he is to some extent discredited before he opens his mouth by the unpleasant implication of his name. But he cannot be wholly dismissed. A certain sour distaste for life is voided through him, something most of us feel at some time or other. If he were not there to give expression to it, we might be tempted to find the picture of life in the forest too sweet. His only action is to interfere in the marriage of Touchstone and Audrey; and this he merely postpones. His effect, whenever he appears, is to deflate: the effect does not last and cheerfulness soon breaks in again. Yet as there is a scale of love, so there is a scale of sadness in the play. It runs down from the duke's compassionate words:

> Thou seest we are not all alone unhappy:
> This wide and universal theatre
> Presents more woeful pageants than the scene
> Wherein we play in,

through Rosalind's complaint, "O, how full of briers is this working-day world," to Jaques's studied refusal to find anything worthy of admiration or love.

One further element in the play I would not wish to stress, because though it is pervasive it is unobtrusive: the constant, natural and easy reference to the Christian ideal of loving kindness, gentleness, pity and humility and to the sanctions which that ideal finds in the commands and promises of religion. In this fantasy world, in which the world of our experience is imaged, this element in experience finds a place with others, and the world is shown not only as a place where we may find happiness, but as a place where both happiness and sorrow may be hallowed. The number of religious references in *As You Like It* has often been commented on, and it is striking when you consider the play's main theme. Many are of little significance and it would be humorless to enlarge upon the significance of the "old religious man" who converted Duke Frederick, or of Ganymede's "old religious uncle." But some are explicit and have a serious, unforced beauty: Orlando's appeal to outlawed men,

> If ever you have look'd on better days,
> If ever been where bells have knoll'd to church . . . ;

Adam's prayer,

> He that doth the ravens feed,
> Yea, providently caters for the sparrow,
> Be comfort to my age!

and Corin's recognition, from St. Paul, that we have to find the way to heaven by doing deeds of hospitality. These are all in character. But the God of Marriage, Hymen, speaks more solemnly than we expect and his opening words with their New Testament echo are more than conventional:

> Then is there mirth in heaven,
> When earthly things made even
> Atone together.

The appearance of the god to present daughter to father and to bless the brides and grooms turns the close into a solemnity, an image of the concord which reigns in Heaven and which Heaven blesses on earth. But this, like much else in the play, may be taken as you like it. There is no need to see any more in the god's appearance with the brides than a piece of pageantry which concludes the action with a graceful spectacle and sends the audience home contented with a very pretty play.

Love's Order and the Judgment of
As You Like It

by John Russell Brown

Shakespeare's history plays are concerned with politics and sociology, but we do not have to be kings or politicians in order to enjoy them; and his comedies, while they are mainly concerned with love and lovers, "hold the mirror up" to more aspects of "nature" than those which are peculiar to a lover's experience. In presenting his ideal of love's wealth in *The Comedy of Errors, The Taming of the Shrew,* and *The Merchant of Venice,* Shakespeare necessarily presented commercial wealth and aspirations as well, and in his exploration of love's truth in *A Midsummer-Night's Dream* and *Much Ado,* he also presented his discoveries about a poet's truth and an actor's. Nor are these contrasts—or dramatic metaphors—seen from a single aspect. The central theme of *Much Ado* is not only expressed through the dialogue and actions of the two pairs of lovers but also through those of Don Pedro, Leonato, Friar Francis, Don John, Borachio, Dogberry, and the watchmen; so in the last scene, when we observe the mazes which the lovers have trod in response to love's imagination, we may also find ourselves reflecting on other mazes, on the vanity of human knowledge and the necessity for it, on the human inability to walk simply, by the shortest route, to the fulfillment of desire. In *The Merchant of Venice* we are shown events through Shylock's eyes as well as through those of the lovers, and in the last act the focus is subtly altered again so that we view Portia and Bassanio as from a distance, against a wider background than that of a mere love story— we judge them as creatures living beneath the stars and we judge their love in comparison with a universal charity.

The comprehensiveness of Shakespeare's mind, his poet's impulse to see the world in a grain of sand, enables us to find our own "nature"

"Love's Order and the Judgment of As You Like It." *From* Shakespeare and His Comedies *by John Russell Brown (London: Methuen & Company Ltd., 1957), pp. 124-8, 135, 141-59. Copyright © 1957 by Methuen & Co. Ltd. Reprinted by permission of the publisher.*

in his "mirror." The comedies, seemingly restricted in their scope to tales of wooing and ideal love, are capable of reflecting the form and pressure of far differing experiences. We have seen how some of the judgments underlying the comedies may be appreciated by following a simple idea about the lover's realization of beauty, or a more individual idea like the concept of love's wealth, but it is also possible to see something of Shakespeare's judgment—of his shaping and ordering of material and of the contrasts and relationships he effects— by following an idea which is more immediately appropriate to other matters than those of love. We may take, as an example, the ideal of order, an ideal which played such a considerable part in shaping the history plays.

✸   ✸   ✸

Shakespeare's history plays, telling the story of England from the reign of John to the crowning of Henry VII, measure the success or failure of kings and nations against an ideal of order.[1] As God was seen as the ruler and judge of all degrees of creation—spiritual, human, animal, vegetable, material—and as each degree was considered to have a clear ascendancy over inferior degrees, so it was considered that the king, "god's deputy," should be the head of the state with its various "members" or degrees in due subservience under him. Political and moral writers found many analogies to this ideal and Shakespeare knew almost all of them; Menenius, in *Coriolanus,* uses the comparison of the head's rule over the body,[2] the Archbishop of Canterbury, in *Henry V,* that a hive of bees where "obedience" or "order" enables many creatures to "work contrariously" yet in harmony and fulfilment,[3] and Henry IV calls on rebels to imitate the constellations and

> . . . *move in that* obedient *orb again*
> *Where you did give a fair and* natural *light,*
> *And be no more an exhaled meteor,*
> *A prodigy of fear and a portent*
> *Of broached mischief to the unborn times.*[4]

Those who rebelled against the king or his officers were "unnatural,"

---

[1] E. M. W. Tillyard's *Shakespeare's History Plays* (1944) traces the influence of this ideal in the plays. His *Elizabethan World Picture* (1943) and A. O. Lovejoy's earlier *The Great Chain of Being* (1936) demonstrate its prevalence and comprehensiveness in Elizabethan thought and feeling.

[2] I. i. 99-164.

[3] I. ii. 183-213.

[4] *Henry IV, Part I,* V. i. 17-21.

or as the Elizabethans often put it, "un-*kind*";[5] they were like animals; "monsters"[6] not men. Without due order a nation would grow to "savagery" and unnatural "wildness";[7] it would be like a diseased body,[8] a "disordered" or unweeded garden,[9] a river overflowing its banks,[10] a "vast confusion" and "tempest."[11]

The ideal of order influenced men's thoughts in many other matters. Each man had to order his faculties as a king ordered a nation; so Prince Hal's personal reformation is described as the unthroning of "Hydra-headed wilfulness,"[12] and Richard II comes to recognize that there should be a "concord" or "music" in men's lives as in the state, a keeping of time and due "proportion."[13] In its widest expression in political, social, human, and religious terms, the ideal of order helped to shape and inform Shakespeare's greatest tragedies, especially *Hamlet, Macbeth,* and *Lear.* Its influence is most apparent in *King Lear* where we are shown a sequence of tyranny, revolt, disorder, judgment, and renewed order, experienced in a nation, in families, and in individuals. Analogies to an ordered state suggested far-ranging images for these actions—images of health, music, wisdom, civilization, constellations, and the natural succession of days and seasons—and Shakespeare used these images to universalize the action of this tragedy, to show in this one "mirror" the whole state of "nature."[14]

As the influence of this ideal of order upon the writing of *King Lear* may be detected by the recurrence of its associated images and similes, so may its influence upon the writing of the comedies.[15] For example, the portrayal of villains called for images of discord and bestiality. When Shylock demands the pound of flesh he is likened to the sea encroaching upon the land, to a wolf, and to "mountain pines . . . fretten with the gusts of heaven."[16] When Shylock demands the right of killing, he justifies it as a right over an animal, not over a man.[17] In *Much Ado,* Don John is "out of *measure*" sad; he "had

[5] Cf., for example, *Henry VI, Part I,* IV. i. 193.
[6] *Henry V,* II. ii. 85.
[7] *Ibid.,* V. ii. 47 ff.
[8] Cf., for example, *Henry VI, Part I,* III. i. 73 and 192-4.
[9] *Richard II,* III. iv. 40-66.
[10] Cf. *King John,* V. iv. 52-7.
[11] *Ibid.,* IV. iii. 152-6.
[12] *Henry V,* I. i. 35-6.
[13] *Richard II,* V. v. 42-8.
[14] Professor John F. Danby has used these images as a key to an appreciation of *King Lear* in his *Shakespeare's Doctrine of Nature* (1949).
[15] G. Wilson Knight's *Shakespearian Tempest* (1932) traces many of these images in the comedies in an attempt to show that an "opposition" between "tempest" and "music" is "the only principle of unity in Shakespeare" (p. 6).
[16] *The Merchant of Venice,* IV. i. 71-80; see also IV. i. 128, 133-8, 217, 287, and 292.
[17] *Ibid.,* IV. i. 69.

rather be a *canker* in a hedge than a rose" in Don Pedro's "grace," and he wishes to use his mouth only to "bite," his "liberty" only to do his own "liking." [18] Images of disorder are especially prevalent in *A Midsummer-Night's Dream,* where they describe the fairy kingdom divided against itself; "brawls" disturb their dances and in consequence:

> . . . *the winds, piping to us in vain,*
> *As in revenge, have suck'd up from the sea*
> *Contagious fogs; which falling in the land*
> *Have every pelting river made so proud*
> *That they have overborne their continents.* . . .
>
> (II. i. 88ff)

Through this "distemperature," or lack of order, even the sequence of seasons has been disturbed. Disorder is again suggested when, in his spite, Oberon plans to make Titania love some loathsome animal.

But even when they are not directly suggested by a villain or a divided kingdom, the images of order and disorder are used in the comedies to picture human relationships. This may be illustrated from the early *Comedy of Errors.* The Antipholi and Dromios accept an habitual order in their relationships with other people as any men might do, but when they are involved in a series of misunderstandings with their twin counterparts the seemingly irrational occurrences suggest a nightmare disorder. . . .

The comedies are chiefly concerned with the establishment of love's order, but, unless we realize the possibility of chaos, the full force of their harmonious conclusions will be lost. Occasionally there are direct remembrances of it: Falstaff's transformation to a Windsor stag—a "beastly fault" (V. v. 10)—is a comic example, and Claudio's outcry that Hero is more "intemperate in her blood" than

> . . . *pamper'd* animals
> *That rage in* savage *sensuality*
>
> (IV. i. 61-2)

is a passionate example. For such glimpses of love's disorder, Shakespeare used images which are able to evoke the whole intellectual and emotional force of the history plays and major tragedies. . . .

* * *

The comedy which culminates in the fullest celebration of the ideal of love's order is *As You Like It.* As "still music" [19] sounds, Hymen

---

[18] I. iii. 1-41.
[19] Folio stage direction.

is drawn mysteriously to this place and time, and links earthly and heavenly harmony:

> *Then is there mirth in heaven*
> *When earthly things made even*
> *Atone together. . . .*

(V. iv. 114ff)

"Atone" means "to achieve unity or concord," [20] and so, when wonder has become more familiar, when the eight lovers have taken hands, and when news has come of the tyrant duke's abdication, music is called for and

> *. . . brides and bridegrooms all,*
> *With measure heap'd in joy, to the measures fall.*

(V. iv. 184-5)

In the circumscribed steps of the dance, the abundance of their joy finds full expression. The exceptional elaboration of this conclusion— its formal groupings, music, song, dancing, and attendant god— suggests that *As You Like It* is informed to an exceptional degree by Shakespeare's ideal of love's order; we may expect to discover a fuller appreciation of its peculiar delightfulness by following throughout its development the images, words, and actions associated with this ideal.

Alone among the comedies, *As You Like It* starts with a single prose speech of over two hundred words; the words are simple enough but the speech is so involved with parenthetical qualifications and elaborations that it has to be delivered slowly and deliberately. Before the play can quicken into action, the audience must hear Orlando reiterate how Oliver, his guardian and eldest brother, keeps him in "servitude," "bars" him the "place of a brother," and treats him as one of his "hinds" or "animals." Oliver's entry interrupts this protestation, but only momentarily, for the two brothers start at once to quarrel in earnest. When Adam, an old servant, begs them, in their father's name, to "be at *accord*" (I. i. 68), Oliver orders him away as an "old dog" (I. i. 85). The whole exchange is a picture of disorder in a family. Left alone, Oliver asks for Charles, the duke's wrestler, and in direct terms—"What's the new news at the new court?" (I. i. 101-2)—calls forth still more direct exposition. There follows a second picture of disorder in society, for, "The old duke," says Charles, "is banished by his younger brother the new duke" (I. ii. 104-5); our attention is turned from a "tyrant brother" in the country, to a "tyrant duke" at the court (I. ii. 300).

It is clear that, in this comedy, Shakespeare is concerned with society

[20] Cf. *O.E.D.*, v. 2.

as well as with love, and at this point anyone who knows Shakespeare's history plays might expect some criticism of these two disorders. It comes at once from Charles, the professional wrestler,[21] who in his dispassionate, professional way tells how "three or four loving lords" have given up "lands and revenues" to go to the forest of Arden and live there with the old duke in "voluntary exile" (I. i. 106-8). Objectively he recounts the common notion of this other court:

> *they say many young gentlemen flock to him every day, and fleet the time carelessly, as they did in the golden world.*
>
> (I. i. 123-5)

After this momentary contrast, the action continues with Oliver persuading Charles to attempt the life of Orlando who intends to wrestle for a prize at court. But when the scene changes there is a further contrast and we are shown Celia, the tyrant duke's daughter, promising Rosalind, the banished duke's daughter, that she will restore all as soon as she is able—she would count herself a *"monster"* if she failed to do this (I. ii. 24).

After these contrasts the tyrant's court is presented more directly. First Touchstone talks, jestingly as befits a clown, of its lack of true honor and wisdom; and then the duke himself enters to watch the wrestling match between Charles and Orlando. Orlando wins but when he says that he is the youngest son of Sir Rowland de Boys, he receives no honor for his victory; although the "world esteem'd" Sir Rowland "honourable," the tyrant had found that he was always his enemy and therefore he cannot welcome the son (I. ii. 237-8). This example of court life comes pat upon Touchstone's moralizing.

The action of the comedy is now well under way, for Rosalind and Orlando have fallen in love, but Shakespeare is still not finished with social disorder. Into the story he found in Lodge's *Rosalynde,* he has already introduced two characters; the first, Touchstone the clown, has been used to comment on the corruptions of the court, and the second, Le Beau the courtier, is now used likewise. As a messenger from the tyrant, he had spoken with marked lack of feeling about the sport which, for his master's entertainment, had killed the three sons of an old father—the incongruity of this entertainment was quickly underlined with a jest from Touchstone—but now, in his own person, he feels such warm friendship for Orlando that he neglects attendance on the duke to counsel him to leave the court. Le Beau recognizes the "malice" of his master; but, as Touchstone had hinted earlier, the "little wit" that he has has been "silenc'd" at court (I. ii. 95); he breaks off his hurried meeting with—

[21] He fights for his professional "honour"; cf. I. i. 137.

> *Sir, fare you well:*
> *Hereafter, in a better world than this,*
> *I shall desire more love and knowledge of you.*
>
> (I. ii. 295-7)

From this world, Rosalind and Celia escape to Arden, and, because she fears the unordered "thieves" of the forest (I. iii. 110-12), Rosalind decides to disguise herself as a page, Ganymede, and they agree to ask Touchstone to accompany them. Thus weakly and foolishly protected, they leave the court's travesty of order and security, going—

> *. . . in content*
> *To* liberty *and not to banishment.*
>
> (I. iii. 139-40)

On this cue the scene changes for the first time to the forest of Arden, and at once our expectations are dashed; it is neither the careless golden world of the people's imagination nor the ruffian world of Rosalind's. We do indeed find contentment there, but it has only been won by *searching* for

> *. . . tongues in trees, books in the running brooks,*
> *Sermons in stones and good in every thing.*
>
> (II. i. 16-17)

There is an "adversity" (II. i. 12), or "stubbornness of fortune," which has to be "translated" into peace and quiet (II. i. 19-20);[22] order and tranquillity are subjective only, and not easily maintained. The banished duke has deliberated so curiously that he is "irked" because the deer, "poor dappled fools" and "native burghers of this desert city," have to be "gored" to provide him with sustenance (II. i. 22-3). This appears to be a new scruple—there's nothing to suggest that he had thought of being a vegetarian while at court—but he is immediately echoed by a jesting report of how Jaques, a lord who seeks to "pierce" to the truth about life in "country, city, court," has found that in killing deer the duke does "more *usurp*" than did his brother who banished him (II. i. 25-63). This short scene concludes with the duke going to hear Jaques' philosophizing. The pastoral and courtly worlds had been compared a thousand times before Shakespeare wrote this play, but here the comparison is unexpected and strangely baffling; it raises issues without answering them, issues clearly related to those

---

[22] The duke's acceptance of the "winter wind" as a counselor that "feelingly" persuades him of what he is (II. 5-11) is a foretaste of Lear upon the heath, and a development of the princess's advice to the king in *Love's Labour's Lost*, V. ii. 802-17.

of earlier scenes by the direct comparison of the "woods" with the "envious court" (II. i. 3-4).

The action returns to the court to show the usurping duke hearing of the princesses' escape and reacting with nervous suspicion and vindictiveness. Then Adam is seen encountering Orlando and persuading him to fly from his brother who is again plotting to take his life. Adam laments in words that partly echo and partly amplify those of Le Beau:

> *O, what a world is this, when what is comely*
> *Envenoms him that bears it.*

> (II. iii. 14-15)

Under Oliver's unnatural tyranny, his "house is but a *butchery*" (II. iii. 27-8), but Orlando swears that he would rather stay there than beg or—

> *. . . with a* base *and* boisterous *sword* enforce
> *A* thievish *living*. . . .

> (II. iii. 32ff)

As Rosalind found comfort in Celia and Touchstone, so Orlando does in Adam who, trusting in the One who "providently caters for the sparrow" (l. 44), gives to his master all the savings of his thrifty, well-ordered youth, and offers to go with him into exile. Like Le Beau and Adam, Orlando now remembers another "world," where order, service, and duty were all respected:

> *O good old man, how well in thee appears*
> *The* constant *service of the antique world,*
> *When service sweat for duty, not for meed!*
> *Thou are not for the fashion of these times,*
> *Where none will sweat but for promotion,*
> *And having that, do* choke *their service up*
> *Even with the having: . . .*

> (II. iii. 56ff)

Together they leave Oliver's tyranny and seek, instead, "some settled low content" (II. iii. 68).

The preliminary pictures of disordered society are now almost complete—there is only one more direct view which comes four scenes later and shows the tyrant sending Oliver "out of doors" to seek his brother while seizing into his own hands the lands and revenues which Oliver had sought to augment. Shakespeare has created these pictures in "primitive" outline and color, a technique which has enabled him to isolate and contrast significant and typical actions. By a series of recurrent words, actions, and images, and by additions to his source, he has shown how generous loyalty and affection cannot purge a disordered world but can at least give to fugitives some measure of personal order and content.

The "primitive" technique of these early scenes has led some critics to think that Shakespeare was only interested in getting to Arden as quickly as possible, but once the action is centered in the forest, he is still not wholly concerned with its delights; repeatedly these early scenes are echoed in theme if not in manner, and their careful contrasts and emphases are made to contribute to the final resolution. For example, the preliminary scene in Arden had stressed the need for a personal acceptance of the "stubbornness of fortune"—the pastoral world was not an easy substitute for the corrupt court—and this is the point which Shakespeare reiterates as each fugitive enters the forest. Rosalind, Celia, and Touchstone are the first to arrive, weary in body and spirit. The clown says frankly that it were better to be at court, while Rosalind, asking the old shepherd Corin for help, hardly dares to hope that such a "desert place" can yield "entertainment" (II. iv. 72). When Corin rejoins that he is a "shepherd to another man," a master of *"churlish* disposition" who

> . . . *little recks to find the way to heaven*
> *By doing deeds of hospitality.* . . . .

> (II. iv. 78ff)

their fears seem confirmed. But Rosalind discovers a kinship with the suffering, amorous shepherd, Silvius, and Corin promises to help them, and at once their spirits rise; Rosalind offers to buy the master's cottage and Celia forgets both her weariness and the unfriendly aspect of Arden—she will "mend" Corin's wages and "willingly could waste" her time in the forest (II. iv. 94-5).

This double aspect of Arden, at one moment forbidding and at the next welcoming, presents problems which no modern scene designer is fully able to solve; indeed its beauty, lying only in the eye of the beholders, cannot be represented objectively. When Orlando enters the forest with Adam, he almost despairs of comfort:

> *If this* uncouth *forest yield any thing savage, I will either be food for it or bring it for food to thee.*

> (II. vi. 6-8)

But if a scene designer listened to Orlando and painted a "desert" (l. 19) visited by "bleak" winds (l. 16), he would have to prepare— the lighting expert would help him—an entirely different setting for the very next moment when we are shown the banished duke and his followers taking their ease and feeding plentifully in the open air.

And even this quick change would not fully serve, for Orlando soon rushes in and tries to force the others to give him food; not only has "bare distress" taken from him all "show of smooth civility" (II. vii. 95-6),[23] but to him the forest is still a "desert inaccessible" and the duke is incongruously at ease under "melancholy boughs" (II. vii. 110-11).

The duke replies to Orlando with true "gentleness," [24] and, having sheathed his sword, Orlando goes to fetch Adam and then joins "the good man's feast," the visible token of order and concord in Arden. Thenceforward he complains no more of Arden's "unkindness"; he lies under its oaks, roams through its glades, and thinks, writes, and talks of Rosalind's perfections:

> *Why should this a* desert *be?*
> *For it is unpeopled? No;*
> *Tongues I'll hang on every tree,*
> *That shall* civil *sayings show:*
> *Some, how brief the life of man*
> *Runs his erring pilgrimage. . . .*
> *Some of violated vows*
> *'Twixt the souls of friend and friend:*
> *But upon the fairest boughs,*
> *Or at every sentence end,*
> *Will I Rosalinda write,*
> *Teaching all that read to know*
> *The quintessence of every sprite*
> *Heaven would in little show. . . .*
> *Heaven would that she these gifts should have,*
> *And I to live and die her slave.*

> (III. ii. 133-62)

The verses are lame, but the reconciliation they attempt to celebrate is complete; if he cannot *find* "tongues in trees, books in the running brooks" by means of the duke's philosophy, he will at least *give* them his own tongue, his "civil sayings"; he can now have order and joy in Arden.

Oliver flying, in his turn, to the forest is threatened by a lioness and a snake, but he is rescued by Orlando, motivated by *"kind*ness, nobler ever than revenge" (IV. iii. 129). This effects a "conversion"

---

[23] Cf. Orlando's earlier boast that he would not "enforce a thievish living" (II. iii. 32-3).

[24] The words "gentleness" (i.e., courtesy, courtliness, *"kind*ness," civilized or ordered sentiment and action), "good manners," "nurture," "civility" are used many times within some thirty lines.

(l. 137) in him, and the two brothers make their peace and go to the "gentle duke" at whose hands Oliver receives "fresh array and entertainment" (ll. 143-4). The earlier pattern is repeated, for Oliver soon falls in love with Celia and is content to resign all his wealth and "live and die a shepherd" in the forest (V. ii. 14); we hear no more of wild beasts or deserts.

Arden is not necessarily or unequivocally the "golden world" of the people's imagination, but "gentleness," "*kind*ness," the duke's philosophy, or the willingness to serve submissively and patiently for love can translate the "stubbornness of fortune" into a sweet and quiet style. This is the point at which the pictures of social disorder and of new-found order in Arden are contrasted and related, and thereby illuminate each other. At court or in Oliver's household, affection and faith could only bring "content" in the "liberty" of banishment; but once in Arden, content is at command: the forest mirrors one's mind; if peace and order are found there, the forest will reflect them.

And at this point too, order and disorder are related to the love stories which are about to take the main focus in the drama. Contentment in love is, like content in Arden, subjective; it is as one's self likes it. Phebe's eyes have power to act against Silvius as "tyrants, butchers, murderers" (III. v. 14), but that is only because Silvius sees her in that way; when she tries to "entame" Ganymede, she is for Rosalind a "tyrant" who "exults" in a power which only Silvius recognizes: " 'Tis not her glass, but you, that flatters her," she tells the youth—

> *And out of you she sees herself more* proper
> *Than any of her lineaments can show her.*
>
> (III. v. 55-6)

This private, subjective truth is sufficient for the lovers, as the subjective order must be for the fugitives in Arden; Silvius can only answer Phebe's refusal with renewed vows of generous service.

And as each of Arden's citizens and each of its lovers finds content in his or her own manner, so both citizens and lovers find it in terms of the "gentleness," service or order which has been neglected in the world outside. For Silvius love is

> *. . . to be all made of faith and service . . .*
> *All adoration, duty, and observance,*
> *All humbleness, all patience and impatience,*
> *All purity, all trial, all observance.*
>
> (V. ii. 95-104)

As in the "antique world" of good order, he "sweats for duty not for meed." And when Phebe finds she has been fooled by the appearance of a man in Ganymede, she accepts the suit of Silvius because of his belief in an order in which she herself believes:

> *Thy* faith *my fancy to thee doth combine.*
>
> (V. iv. 156)

Oliver and Celia establish their mutual content more rapidly and confidently, but it is still in terms of order; as Caesar established his kingdoms, so they both "came, saw, and overcame" (V. ii. 35). Rosalind and Orlando had met for the first time at court, but their love was not fully expressed there. They had done what they could—Rosalind had given him a favor to wear and both had confessed that they were "thrown down," "overthrown," disordered by a new "master" and new duties of service[25]—yet more was expressed in their hesitations than in words or deeds, and it is only in Arden that they learn the full strength of their new order, of their mutual defeat and mastery. In the forest they learn to make their love explicit in the very words by which Silvius vows his service, observance, and faith.[26] On one level the story of Rosalind and Orlando is easily appreciated; but it should be seen in the context of the whole play, of the tyrannies outside Arden, of the subjective content which can be won within Arden, and of the other love stories; all these are informed by Shakespeare's ideal of order and all these contribute to the implicit judgment of the play, and to the full significance of any part of it.

Arden's pleasures and love's order do not recommend themselves to all comers. Touchstone does not readily give way to such enthusiasms: he is "Nature's natural" (I. ii. 52) who cares not for his "spirits" if his legs are not "weary" (II. iv. 2-3). The excitement of a lover, the zeal of a scholar, the business of a lawyer do not affect, for him, the pace of Time;[27] for him, Time travels regularly:

> *'Tis but an hour ago since it was nine,*
> *And after one hour more 'twill be eleven;*
> *And so, from hour to hour, we ripe and ripe,*
> *And then, from hour to hour, we rot and rot. . . .*
>
> (II. vii. 24-7)

Determined to treat a spade only as a spade, Touchstone will not be carried away by any subjective idealization of life in Arden:

> *in respect of itself, it is a good life; but in respect that it is a shepherd's life, it is naught. . . .*
>
> (III. ii. 13ff)

---

[25] I. ii. 262, 266, and 271-2.

[26] Cf. V. ii. 89-108; the addition of this chorus of lovers is among the most significant modifications to Lodge's *Rosalynde.*

[27] Cf. III. ii. 320-51.

In the affairs of love he reckons, like Costard, on the "simplicity of
man";[28] he notices the "strange capers" which lovers run into (II. iv.
55), but he quickly accounts for such vagaries:

> *If a hart do lack a hind,*
> *Let him seek out Rosalind.*
> *If the cat will after kind,*
> *So be sure will Rosalind.* . . .

(III. ii. 107ff)

Yet once Touchstone finds Audrey his attitude changes; the desire
to possess involves him, by degrees, in the mutual order of love. The
first time we see them together, he is offering to "fetch up" her goats
and is already impatient of Time, questioning "Am I the man yet?
doth my simple feature *content* you?" (III. iii. 1-4). He cannot con-
template his actions without misgivings, but he rallies his courage:

> . . . *As horns are odious, they are necessary* . . . *as a walled town is*
> *more* worthier *than a village, so is the forehead of a married man more*
> honourable *than the bare brow of a bachelor; and by how much defence*
> *is better than no skill, by so much is a horn more precious than to want.*

(III. iii. 48-62)

When Jaques tells him that Sir Oliver Martext can only wed them
like badly joined wainscot, Touchstone professes himself content, for,
in due time, this will give him the better excuse to leave his wife.
But he is further in than he admits, and, to Audrey's surprise, he fails
to take advantage of Sir Oliver but goes with Jaques to find a "good
priest that can tell . . . what marriage is" (ll. 86-7). He now remembers, not merely that "cat will after kind," but also something which
is above man's apparent "simplicity"; he recollects that

> *As the ox hath his* bow, . . . *the horse his* curb *and the falcon her* bells,
> *so man hath his desires; and as pigeons bill, so* wedlock *will be nibbling.*

(III. iii. 80-3)

The "yoke," "curb," or order of love also seems to be "necessary,"
even for a man of "a fearful heart."

Touchstone falls in with the ordered dance of the lovers as best he
may. First he jousts with William, a youth of the forest who lays claim
to Audrey, and, asserting his new-found possessiveness, routs the com-
placent, good-natured clown. Then he is ready to press in "amongst
the rest of the country copulatives" (V. iv. 57-8). Knowing that "marriage binds and blood breaks," he expects to "swear and to forswear"
(ll. 58-60); but he makes what show he can. Audrey may not cut a

---

[28] *Love's Labour's Lost,* I. i. 219.

fine figure in the eyes of other people but love is ever "as you like it"; "a poor virgin, sir," he explains, "an ill-favoured thing, sir, but mine own" (ll. 60-1). And as he is now disposed to dignify any complaisance with the formality of honor and good manners, so he commands Audrey—and his concern for this draws laughter from everyone—to "bear" her "body more seeming" (l. 72).[29] Touchstone may yet find the "pearl" in his "foul oyster"; at least he knows something of the terms—the mutual order of love—on which such treasure is discovered.

By adding Touchstone to the story that he had found in Lodge's *Rosalynde*, Shakespeare has emphasized the implicit judgment of this play; by contrast and relationship with other characters, Touchstone illuminates the main theme in each of its three branches—social disorder, Arden's subjective order, and love's order. And Shakespeare's preoccupation with these ideas becomes even clearer when we notice that Jaques, his other major addition to Lodge, is used in the same threefold manner.

Jaques' talent is for the exposure of disorder, not the affirmation of order; we first hear a report of his whimsically extravagant denunciation of the duke's "tyranny" over the deer, and then we see him "sucking" melancholy from Amiens' song, as "a weasel sucks eggs" (II. v. 12-14). Jaques rightly uses a destructive image to describe his pleasure, for he finds no joy in the song's harmony nor in its simple, complaisant reconciliation with Arden:

> *Under the greenwood tree*
> *Who loves to lie with me,*
> *And turn his merry note*
> *Unto the sweet bird's throat,*
> *Come hither, come hither, come hither:*
> *Here shall he see*
> *No enemy*
> *But winter and rough weather.*

                                                    (II. v. 1-8)

The "young"[30] foresters join in with Amiens' second stanza but Jaques thinks of the "grossness," the lack of complexity, which their song represents. He offers another stanza of his own:

> *If it do come to pass*
> *That any men turn ass,*
> *Leaving his wealth and ease,*

---

[29] For Shakespeare's age, "seeming" meant suitably, becomingly, beseemly.
[30] Cf. I. i. 123.

> *A stubborn will to please,*
> *Ducdame, ducdame, ducdame:*
> *Here shall he see*
> *Gross fools as he,*
> *An if he will come to me.*

                                                       (II. v. 52-9)

Observing the circle in which the young men have gathered to ask
what "ducdame" means, Jaques uses it as a token of their easy-going
acceptance of order in Arden: " 'Tis a Greek invocation," he explains,
"to call fools into a circle" (ll. 61-2).

Jaques will not risk being a fool on his own account—he prefers to
rail against others—but he feels a kinship with the clown Touchstone
who sees life as a mere "simplicity" of ripening and rotting. He is
at once ambitious for a fool's license to speak his mind and so, as he
believes,—

> *. . . through and through*
> *Cleanse the* foul *body of the* infected *world.*

                                                       (II. vii. 59-60)

Given his liberty he would sing no song, but rail against disorder,
against the city woman who bears the "cost of princes on *unworthy*
shoulders" and against the upstart courtier of *"basest* function" (ll.
74-82). When Orlando enters, desperate with hunger, Jaques has only
"reason" to offer as a cure (ll. 100-1);[31] and then, while Orlando goes
to fetch Adam at the duke's invitation, he proceeds to amplify Touchstone's wisdom and to speak of the seven ages of man as of a mere
mutation in response to time's ordering—of man's own ordering
vision, he makes no account. At this point Shakespeare fully demon-
strates Jaques' limitations, for as soon as he has called old age a
"second childishness and mere oblivion" (l. 165), Orlando re-enters
with the aged Adam whose "constant service" has made him the
"venerable burden" which the duke at once recognizes. Following this
reminder of all that Jaques had forgotten, Amiens sings of man's
ingratitude; respect for virtue is not forgetfulness.

Jaques' negative, reasonable, and unenthusiastic attitude towards
men and society, which decries disorder but neglects to praise and
appreciate such order as men have achieved, is matched by his attitude
to lovers. With Orlando, conversation is almost impossible. Jaques
reproves him for "marring" the trees by "writing love-songs in their
barks," and Orlando reproves Jaques for reading them so "ill-fa-

---

[31] There may be a pun on reason/raisin for Orlando has just demanded some
fruit; such a pun would tend to emphasize the single word, the rational purgative
that is Jaques' only medicine.

vouredly" (III. i. 276-9). Jaques does not like the name of Rosalind, and Orlando does not defend it; these matters are "as you like it" and there was "no thought of pleasing [him] when she was christened" (ll. 283-4). Jaques invites him to rail "against our mistress the world and all our misery," and Orlando, mindful of another mistress, answers that he will "chide no breather in the world" but himself, against whom he knows "most faults" (ll. 295-300). Orlando's love leads him into absurdities which appear as "faults" to others; but they are faults that Orlando would not change for the "best virtue" that Jaques can boast of (ll. 301-2).

Jaques has more to say to Touchstone, for he must denounce the iniquities of Martext; but with Rosalind he can only once more manifest his ignorance of love's inward order and joy. He is neither scholar, musician, courtier, soldier, lawyer, nor lover; and he feels none of their emotions—he merely contemplates their exploits and failures, and gains a "most humorous sadness" (IV. i. 20). This is his only possession. Orlando interrupts his talk with Rosalind, or rather with Ganymede, by addressing the seeming boy with "Good day and happiness, dear Rosalind"; to Jaques this is doubly nonsense and he leaves, baffled by their mutual, private pleasure.

When the duke is restored to his true place in society by the sudden conversion of his tyrant brother, Jaques cannot join the dance which celebrates the new order of the lovers; unappeased, he must seek more matter for his contemplation. But having seen them all endure "shrewd days and nights" (V. iv. 179), he accepts this as testimony of their inward virtues, and, for the first time in the play, sees promise of order, not of disorder. He speaks formally and in due order—to the duke:

> *You to your former honour I bequeath;*
> *Your patience and your virtue well deserves it:*

then to Orlando, Oliver, and Silvius in turn, dismissing them:

> *You to a love that your true faith doth merit:*
> *You to your land and love and great allies:*
> *You to a long and well-deserved bed.*
>
> (V. iv. 192-6)

For Touchstone he foresees "wrangling"; for the clown has only given proof of "victual" for some two months of "loving voyage" with Audrey (V. iv. 197-8). This is a rational appraisement of their several chances of creating love's order in the more complex, less subjective, world of society at large.

A detached critic who rails at the follies or "disorders" of others

sounds a tiresome character for any comedy; but even when Jaques
criticizes those who affirm individual visions of order, the effect on
them is only to add to their happiness; his "sullen fits" (II. i. 67) are
sport for the philosophical duke, his encounters with Rosalind and
Orlando encourage them to be more confident in their own happiness,
and his mockery of the young foresters for "conquering" the deer,
sends them singing through the forest.[32] His strictures on corrupt
society can give pleasure by the seasoned wit with which he, like a
true satirist, affirms the value of order by recognizing and describing
disorder; as he himself says, his "sadness" is one, limited, kind of
"good" (IV. i. 7). Without Jaques, *As You Like It* would be a far less
subtle play, for besides showing the limitations of his own disinterested
judgment, he makes us aware of the limitations of subjective order
and content; he shows us that the philosophical duke is "too disputable"
for some company (II. v. 36), that the young foresters are content
because they are easily so, that Orlando does not care to mend his
most obvious absurdities. And indirectly Jaques affirms the complexity
of love's order; for as the couples come together at the close of the
play, he reminds us that they are not merely servants of each other's
excellencies, but also "couples . . . coming to the Ark," some of them
very "strange beasts" (V. iv. 36-7).

To follow Jaques through the play is to become aware of Shakespeare's preoccupation with the ideal of order in society, in Arden,
and in love, and of the subtlety and range of his consequent judgments. But Jaques alone cannot suggest the light-footed gaiety, the
warmth, and the confidence with which this comedy is written. Some
of these qualities derive from the apparently easy interplay between
the varied and individually conceived characters; for example, the
absurdly single-minded Silvius is first introduced talking to the simply
and sensibly satisfied Corin, and overheard by Rosalind and Touchstone; and then, later, Touchstone and Corin meet and compare their
individual "simplicities." But the play's generosity and confidence
spring chiefly from the characterization of Rosalind. She insures that
Shakespeare's ideal of love's order is not presented as a cold theorem;
in her person, love's doubts and faith, love's obedience and freedom,
coexist in delightful animation.

The lively characterization of Rosalind is not an added, irrelevant
pleasure, but arises from, and continually illuminates, the thematic
structure of the whole play. This is perhaps Shakespeare's greatest
triumph in *As You Like It:* from the moment she is disordered by
the claims of love to the moment when she makes Orlando reiterate
their "compact" (V. iv. 5) for the last, unnecessary time, she invites

[32] Cf. IV. ii.

our understanding as well as our enthusiasm. She delights to "play the knave" with Orlando (III. ii. 314-15), for the more she casts doubts upon whether he is truly "sick" of an unsatisfied love, the more assurance she receives that he is indeed so, and the more outrageously she pictures women, the more strongly he affirms his faith in her own virtue. Yet while his faith permits her to enjoy this freedom, she is careful to offer no more alluring "cure" for his "sickness" than the prospect of living "in a nook merely monastic" (III. ii. 440-1). Love's order has its justice, and Rosalind must pay for the advantage she delights to take; Orlando, protected by the belief that she is Ganymede, can come "within an hour" of his promise and be quite easy in mind (IV. i. 42-3); but for Rosalind, to "break but a part of the thousandth part of a minute" has its torments. She may "disable" all the fabled heroics of other lovers; but that is only because her own love is too great to be spoken, because she "cannot be out of the sight of Orlando" (IV. i. 223-4).

In the two central scenes between Orlando and Rosalind, Shakespeare shows us the growing assurance of their mutual love, its generosity, truth, and order. And at the close of the play, he directs that they should take hands in the forefront of the other lovers and, after the final dance affirming the creation of mutual order, that they should go back with the duke to the court, away from purely subjective content—they go to play their part on the great stage of society and to affirm order and harmony there.

And then Rosalind steps forward:

> *It is not the fashion to see the lady the epilogue; but it is no more unhandsome than to see the lord the prologue. . . .*

She will not beg for applause for the play; her "way is to conjure":

> *I charge you, O women, for the love you bear to men, to like as much of this play as please you: and I charge you, O men, for the love you bear to women—as I perceive by your simpering, none of you hates them—that between you and the women the play may please.*

"Between the men and the women" the play *can* please; for it mirrors the "mutual ordering" of love. If we answer its "conjuration," we shall, consciously or unconsciously, be "pleased" with its ideal of harmony. We may, of course, allow the trick to retain all its mystery, but if we wish, by tracing the implicit judgments of the play, we may realize that it succeeds not merely by some sleight of hand, but also by reason of the ideals which inform it.

"No Clock in the Forest":
Time in *As You Like It*

by Jay L. Halio

In *As You Like It* Shakespeare exploits timelessness as a convention of the pastoral ideal along with other conventions taken from pastoralism; but unlike his treatment, say, of Silvius and Phebe, his treatment of time is not so thoroughly satirical. Although neither will quite do, timelessness in Arden (on the whole) contrasts favorably to the time-consciousness of court and city life that Touchstone, for example, brings to the forest. In addition, timelessness links life in Arden with the ideal of an older, more gracious way of life that helps regenerate a corrupt present.

I

Orlando's first speech immediately voices several aspects of the time theme. Speaking to Adam, he recalls his father's will and its provision that Oliver, the eldest son, should educate the younger brothers. This Oliver has failed to do, at least with respect to Sir Rowland's youngest son; but despite his enforced rusticity, Orlando reveals an innate gentility so wonderful that even his tyrannical brother is brought to remark: "Yet he's gentle, never schooled, and yet learned, full of noble device, of all sorts enchantingly beloved. . . ." [1] These innate qualities derive directly from old Sir Rowland, for the identification between Orlando and his father, as we shall see, is repeatedly and pointedly made. Moreover, Orlando twice remarks in this scene that it is his father's spirit within him that prompts him to revolt against his present humiliation—a revelation that has more than ordinary implications later.

" 'No Clock in the Forest': Time in As You Like It," by Jay L. Halio. From SEL (Studies in English Literature, 1500-1900), II (1962), 197-207. Copyright © 1962 by Rice University Press. Reprinted by permission of the publisher.

[1] I. i. 172-4. Quotations are from G. B. Harrison's *Shakespeare: The Complete Works* (New York, 1952).

Unlike his counterpart, Sir John of Bordeaux, in Lodge's *Rosalynde,* Sir Rowland de Boys is dead before the play opens; but his memory is kept studiously alive. In the opening lines of Lodge's novel we can get some idea of what he stood for:

> There dwelled adjoining to the city of Bordeaux a knight of most honorable parentage, whom fortune had graced with many favors, and nature honored with sundry exquisite qualities, so beautified with the excellence of both, as it was a question whether fortune or nature were more prodigal in deciphering the riches of their bounties. Wise he was, as holding in his head a supreme conceit of policy, reaching with Nestor into the depth of all civil government; and to make his wisdom more gracious, he had that *salem ingenii* and pleasant eloquence that was so highly commended in Ulysses: his valor was no less than his wit, nor the stroke of his lance no less forcible than the sweetness of his tongue was persuasive; for he was for his courage chosen the principal of all the Knights of Malta.

But we need not go outside the play to discover what Sir Rowland represents. Adam, the old retainer of the de Boys household and himself a living reminder of the former age, provides some important clues. When Oliver apparently consents to his brother's departure, he throws Adam out, too:

> *Oliver.* Get you with him, you old dog.
> *Adam.* Is "old dog" my reward? Most true, I have lost teeth in your service. God be with my old master! He would not have spoke such a word.

(I. i. 85-9)

Later, when Adam warns Orlando to run from Oliver's treachery and even offers his life's savings—and his life—to assist in the escape, Orlando recognizes the gesture for what it is—the product of a gracious ideal:

> O good old man, how well in thee appears
> The constant service of the antique world,
> When service sweat for duty, not for meed!
> Thou art not for the fashion of these times,
> Where none will sweat but for promotion,
> And having that do choke their service up
> Even with the having. It is not so with thee.

(II. iii. 56-62)

The two dukes also furnish evidence of the esteem in which Sir Rowland was universally held: Duke Frederick, villainously, found him an enemy; but Duke Senior (to Rosalind's evident gratification) "loved Sir Rowland as his soul" (I. ii. 247). Orlando, who functions in

the play partly to bear out the spirit of his father, naturally attracts
similar feelings. It is not for nothing that he attaches to himself
repeatedly the clumsy-naïve epithet "old Sir Rowland's youngest son";
besides, his name is both an anagram of Rowland and its Italian translation.[2] The predicament in which the young man eventually discovers himself will test his true mettle and, more importantly, the
worth of all that he and his name may symbolize. Adam awakens in
him some sense of his plight when Orlando returns home after throwing Charles the wrestler:

> O you memory
> Of old Sir Rowland! Why, what make you here?
> Why are you so virtuous? Why do people love you?
> And wherefore are you gentle, strong, and valiant?
> Why would you be so fond to overcome
> The bonny prizer of the humorous Duke?
> Your praise is come too swiftly home before you.
> Know you not, master, to some kind of men
> Their graces serve them but as enemies?
> No more do yours. Your virtues, gentle master,
> Are sanctified and holy traitors to you.
> Oh, what a world is this when what is comely
> Envenoms him that bears it!
>
> (II. iii. 3-15)

Orlando's world of court and city is a far different world from his
father's. It is a perverse world, where brother plots against brother
and virtues become "sanctified and holy traitors." It is a world ruled
over by the usurping Frederick (the "new" duke), who banishes his
elder brother (the "old" duke) and keeps his niece only so long as
convenience allows. When he fears Rosalind as a threat to the fame
and popularity of his own daughter, he drives her out also—just as
Oliver plans to kill the brother he fears he can no longer suppress.
In short, it is a world based on expediency and the lust for power
(III. i. 15-18), not a brave new world, but a degenerate new one.
With no obligation to tradition—to the past—it is ruthless in its self-
assertion. But although this "new" world may banish its principal
threats, Rosalind and Orlando, it does not thus destroy them (we are,

---

[2] Possibly a reason for Shakespeare's changing the names from his source. My
colleague, Professor Celeste Wright, suggests an ironic play upon the expression
"(to give) a Roland for an Oliver" (see *OED*) as another reason, especially as
the allusion to the *Chanson de Roland*, from which this expression derives, is
appropriate to ideals promulgated in the play. Cf. *Henry VI, Part I*, I. ii. 30. For
the change of surname to *de Boys*, see below.

after all, in the realm of romantic comedy). In the timeless pastoral world of the Forest of Arden, where past and present merge, they find refuge and there flourish.

II

The first mention of the life led by Duke Senior and his fellows in the Forest of Arden occurs early in the play in the dialogue between Charles and Oliver. Oliver has decided to use the wrestler to rid himself of Orlando (thus perverting the intention of Charles's visit), but first he inquires into the "new news at the new Court" (I. i. 101). Charles recounts what Oliver already knows: The new duke has driven out the old duke, and a number of lords have voluntarily accompanied him into exile. For no apparent reason, Oliver next inquires into Rosalind's position, and then asks where the old duke will live. Charles replies:

> They say he is already in the Forest of Arden, and a many merry men with him; and there they live like the old Robin Hood of England. They say many young gentlemen flock to him every day, and fleet their time carelessly as they did in the golden world.
>
> (I. i. 120-5)

Here Oliver abruptly changes the subject to the next day's wrestling match. Now, merely as dramatic exposition this dialogue is at least ingenuous—if not downright clumsy. Obviously it must serve another function to justify itself; that is, by describing the conflict between the two dukes, it provides a parallel to the decisive quarrel between Orlando and Oliver that has just taken place. The inversion of roles played by the younger and older brothers is merely a superficial variation of the plot; the point is to suggest an alignment between Duke Senior and Sir Rowland de Boys, between the "golden world" and the "antique world," which coalesce in the fabulous Robin Hood life now led by the banished duke. Should we require any further evidence of this significance, the change in Sir Rowland's name from its source is clear enough. The anagram *Rowland-Orlando* has already been explained, but the change from *de Bordeaux* is otherwise meaningful: *de Boys* is simply *de Bois,* "of the forest." Elizabethan spelling commonly substitutes *y* for *i,* as everyone knows, but the pronunciation is the same. While older editors, such as Malone and Dyce, modernize the spelling (without comment), more recent ones prefer the spelling of the Folios, a practice that tends to obscure the reference. And Dover

Wilson's note, recording the fact that the de Boyses were an old Arden family, gives us more light than it perhaps suspects—or intends.[3]

Lest there be any mistake about the kind of forest in which Duke Senior and (later) Orlando, Rosalind, and the others find themselves, we must listen carefully to the duke's first speech (II. i. 1 ff).[4] Its theme is "Sweet are the uses of adversity"; only in this way can he and his followers discover "tongues in trees, books in the running brooks / . . . and good in everything." Here, unlike the conventional pastoral, others besides unrequited lovers may feel the shrewdness of the winter wind; shepherds will confess to smelling of sheep dip; and a Sir Oliver Martext is available for weddings as well as Hymen. The forest may be enchanted—the appearance of a god is only the least subtle indication that it is—but the enchantment is of an unusual kind; the forest still admits of other, qualifying realities. For the right apprehension of a natural, humane order of life, which emerges as Shakespeare's standard, takes account of both the ideal (what should or could be) and the actual (what is).[5] By contrast, the standard of life in court and city is unnatural insofar as it stifles the ideal aspirations of the human imagination and sinks to the level of a crude, animal existence. If Duke Senior finally returns along with the others to his dukedom (despite his earlier assertion that he would not change his "life exempt from public haunt"), he returns not only because his dukedom is ready to receive him, but also (we must infer) because he is prepared to resume his proper role. Tempered by adversity, his virtue matures. To provide this temper, or balance, is the true function of the forest, its real "magic." Neither the duke nor anyone else who comes to Arden emerges the same.[6]

The trip to the forest is itself exhausting and fraught with danger. Rosalind and her little company are quite unable to take another step. Similarly, Adam is close to expiring when he arrives with Orlando. But on each occasion the forest at once works its charm. Corin and Silvius are at hand to entertain Rosalind and her friends and to provide them with a gentle welcome and a home. At the end of the scene even the fainting Celia quickens to remark, "I like this place, / And willingly could waste my time in it" (II. iv. 94). Orlando, seeking food

[3] "There appears to have been a family named de Boys which held the manor of Weston-in-Arden for several generations during the middle ages (French, *Shakespeareana Geneologica,* 1869, p. 316)," New Cambridge ed., p. 110.
[4] See also V. iv. 173-81.
[5] Harold Jenkins develops Shakespeare's "art of comic juxtaposition" in an excellent article, *"As You Like It," Shakespeare Survey,* VIII (1955), 40-51; reprinted above. Jenkins notes that "it is a mark of Shakespeare's mature comedy that he permits . . . criticism of his ideal world in the very center of it" (p. 45).
[6] Compare Jaques, who, lacking this balance, remains.

in what he calls an "uncouth" desert (II. vi. 6), comes upon the banquet
of the banished duke. Showing the valor of his heritage, he opposes
single-handed the entire host of the duke and his men. Under the
conventions of this romance, this show of valor is not quixotic—it fits
rather with Orlando's defeat of Charles. But, although hardly despised
(except by Jaques), it is misdirected; and Orlando is made to recognize
the code that here reigns:

> Speak you so gently? Pardon me, I pray you.
> I thought that all things had been savage here,
> And therefore put I on the countenance
> Of stern commandment. But whate'er you are
> That in this desert inaccessible,
> Under the shade of melancholy boughs,
> Lose and neglect the creeping hours of time,
> If ever you have looked on better days,
> If ever been where bells have knolled to church,
> If ever sat at good man's feast,
> If ever from your eyelids wiped a tear
> And know what 'tis to pity and be pitied,
> Let gentleness my strong enforcement be.
> In the which hope I blush, and hide my sword.
>
> (II. vii. 106-19)

Gentleness joins with gentleness; golden world merges with antique
world—at least through their modern representatives. If the parvenu
at first mistakes the appearance of his surroundings, he is soon in-
structed: this is no ordinary forest. At the same time, he reminds us
of what civilization *might* be like, or once was. Certainly he perceives
another aspect of his new environment accurately, one he will quickly
cultivate: the meaninglessness of time in the forest.

III

For unlike the life of the court and the city, "men fleet the time
carelessly" in Arden, as Charles earlier remarked. Here are no power-
seekers like Oliver and Duke Frederick, impatient to rid themselves
of encumbrances (I. i. 124, I. iii. 152 ff), but men who love to lie under
the greenwood tree seeking—only the food they eat. Appropriately,
this casualness is the theme of many of their songs. Touchstone's comment on the last—"I count it but lost time to hear such a foolish song"
(V. iii. 40)—briefly expresses the opposing attitude brought from court
into the forest. The attitude is shared by the malcontent Jaques, his
fellow satirist, and in some respects by Rosalind. Touchstone is, in fact,

the play's timekeeper, as Harold Jenkins has called him (p. 49), and his most extended disquisition on time is fittingly recounted by Jaques:

> . . . he drew a dial from his poke,
> And looking on it with lack-lustre eye,
> Says very wisely, "It is ten o'clock.
> Thus we may see," quoth he, "how the world wags.
> 'Tis but an hour ago since it was nine,
> And after one hour more 'twill be eleven;
> And so, from hour to hour, we ripe and ripe,
> And then, from hour to hour, we rot and rot;
> And thereby hangs a tale."

(II. vii. 20-8)

Later in the same scene Jaques *in propria persona* also "morals on the time" in his speech on the Seven Ages of Man, calling our attention to the broader divisions of time's progress and pageant. Between these speeches, it should be noted, occur Orlando's entrance and his words, quoted above, on the neglect of time by the duke and his foresters. Clearly, Shakespeare throughout the play contrasts the timelessness of the forest world with the time-ridden preoccupations of court and city life, but here the juxtaposition is both dramatically and thematically emphasized. For the court and city habitués, time is a measured progress to the grave—or worse! But for the foresters, time is merely "the stream we go a-fishing in" (to borrow the phrase of a later pastoralist).[7] Neither attitude, of course, will quite do in this sublunary world; hence, to present a more balanced view of time—as of love, pastoralism, and poetry—Shakespeare uses the dialectic characteristic of this play and centers it upon his hero and heroine.

For Rosalind's awareness of time, however related to the preoccupation imported from the "outside" world, is different from Touchstone's obsession with "riping and rotting."[8] It is, partly, the awareness of a girl in love and impatient for the attentions of her lover, a healthy consciousness that recalls Juliet's except as the former is undarkened by tragic fate. But her awareness has further implications. When she and Orlando first meet in the forest, their dialogue, appropriately enough, is itself about time. Rosalind's question, "I pray you, what

---

[7] Henry David Thoreau, *Walden*, ed. Brooks Atkinson (New York, 1937), p. 88. The opposition also appears structurally—in the "frame" provided by the scenes of the first act and the imminent departure from Arden at the end of the play, and (as Jenkins points out, p. 44) in certain brief scenes of Acts II and III that serve to remind us of what is still happening at Oliver's house and at the court of Duke Frederick.

[8] See Helge Kökeritz, *Shakespeare's Pronunciation* (New Haven, 1953), pp. 58-9, for the punning significance of this passage.

is't o'clock?", although banal, suits the occasion; for despite her
boast that she will speak like a saucy lackey, she is momentarily confused by confronting Orlando and scarcely knows how to begin.
What follows in her account of time's "divers paces" (III. ii. 317-51),
however, is something more than a verbal smokescreen to help her
collect her wits, detain her lover, and make sure he keeps coming
back: it is a development of Jaques's Seven Ages speech with important
thematic variations. Jaques's speech describes a man in his time playing many parts and suggests that his speed, or "pace," will vary along
with his role; the series of vignettes illustrates the movement of a person *in* time. Rosalind not only adds appreciably to Jaques's gallery,
but showing profounder insight, she shifts the emphasis from the movement *of a person,* to the movement *of time* as apprehended, for example, by the young maid "between the contract of her marriage and
the day it is solemniz'd. If the interim be but a se'ennight, Time's pace
is so hard that it seems the length of seven years." In this way, she
more thoroughly accounts for *duration,* or the perception of time,
which, unlike Jaques's portrait of our common destiny, is not the
same for everyone.

IV

Naturally, Rosalind is most concerned with the perception of time
by the lover, and here her behavior is in marked contrast to Orlando's.
Quite literally—and like any fiancée, or wife—she is Orlando's timekeeper. When he fails to keep his appointments, she suffers both pain
and embarrassment (III. iv) that are relieved only by the greater follies
of Silvius and Phebe that immediately follow. When he finally does
turn up an hour late—as if to dramatize his belief that "there's no
clock in the forest" (III. ii. 319)—Rosalind rebukes him severely:

> *Rosalind.* Why, how now, Orlando? Where have you been all this while?
> You a lover? An you serve such another trick, never come in my sight
> more.
> *Orlando.* My fair Rosalind, I come within an hour of my promise.
> *Rosalind.* Break an hour's promise in love? He that will divide a minute
> into a thousand parts and break but a part of the thousand part of a
> minute in the affairs of love, it may be said of him that Cupid hath
> clapp'd him o' th' shoulder, but I'll warrant him heart-whole.
> *Orlando.* Pardon me, dear Rosalind.
> *Rosalind.* Nay, an you be so tardy, come no more in my sight. I had as
> lief be woo'd of a snail.

(IV. i. 38-52)

Rosalind's time-consciousness goes beyond the mere moment: She

knows the history of love—witness her speech on Troilus and Leander
(IV. i. 94-108)—and she predicts its future, as she warns Orlando of
love's seasons after marriage (IV. i. 143-49). Her ardent impulse is
thus in comic juxtaposition with her realistic insight, just as Orlando's
"point-device" attire and time-unconsciousness comically contrast with
his rimes and other protestations of love.

In this fashion we arrive at the theme's center, or balance. If Orlando, as we have seen, is an agent of regeneration, he appears through
his forgetfulness of time to be in some danger of not realizing his
functions. Were it not for Rosalind, he might, like Silvius, linger
through an eternity of unconsummated loving;[9] certainly, like the
duke, he feels in the forest no urgency about his heritage—at least
not until he comes upon his brother sleeping beneath an ancient oak
tree and menaced by a starved lioness (the symbolism is obvious).
Oliver's remarkable conversion after his rescue and his still more
remarkable engagement to Celia pave the way for Rosalind's resolution of the action; for under the pressure of his brother's happiness,
Orlando can play at games in love no longer. And despite the play's
arbitrary finale—Duke Frederick's conversion and the end of exile,
in all of which she has had no hand—nevertheless, it is again Rosalind
who has had an important share in preparing the principals for this
chance. Like her less attractive counterpart Helena in *All's Well That
Ends Well,* she remains a primary agent for the synthesis of values that
underlies regeneration in Shakespeare's comedy. At the very outset
we see her, the daughter of Duke Senior at the court of Duke Frederick,
as a link between two worlds, not unlike Orlando's representative
linking of two generations.[10] In love, she is realistic rather than cynical,
but not without a paradoxical—and perfectly human—romantic bias.
So, too, with regard to time she moves with Orlando to a proper
balance of unharried awareness. For all of these functions—as for
others—the timeless world of the forest, with its complement of aliens,
serves as a haven; but more importantly, it serves as a school.

Neither the extremes of idealism nor those of materialism, as they
are variously represented, emerge as "the good life" in *As You Like It.*
That life is seen rather as a mean of natural human sympathy educated
—since that is a major theme in the play—by the more acceptable
refinements of civilization (II. vii) and the harsh realities of existence
("winter and rough weather"). The "antique world" stands for a
timeless order of civilization still in touch with natural human sym-

[9] Cf. Jenkins, p. 48.

[10] In his highly perceptive analysis of *The Winter's Tale,* S. L. Bethell shows
later developments of these aspects of the time theme in Shakespeare, explicitly
linking them in several important ways to *As You Like It.* See *"The Winter's
Tale": A Study* (London, 1947), p. 27, passim.

pathy that, under the "new" regime (while it lasted), had been forced underground. To the forest, the repository of natural life devoid of artificial time barriers, the champions of regeneration repair in order to derive new energy for the task before them. There they find refuge, gain strength, learn—and return.

What Shakespeare Did to *Rosalynde*

by Marco Mincoff

The study of sources seems of recent years and after a period of neglect, to be coming to the fore again. And fortunately so. For comparison with the source, by giving us a definite standard of measurement, can help us to a clearer insight into a writer's intentions and methods of work than any analysis in the void; in a purely original work it may be difficult to decide what is fortuitous and what intentional, but any deviation from the source, any addition, omission or alteration, immediately imposes on us the question of the underlying purpose. Yet it must be admitted that too many earlier studies of sources tended to overlook this all-important point, to limit themselves to an enumeration of borrowings and of the material actually taken over, and to regard any sort of borrowing as an "influence"; and by their cumulative effect they seemed to stress the writer's lack of originality rather than his creative powers in reshaping old material. Above all, by stressing the positive side of the borrowings they often failed to make a satisfactory use of the instrument to hand; for an author's rejections are often as important as his actual borrowings.

From this point of view it is perhaps rather odd that two recent comparisons of *As You Like It* with its source both regard Shakespeare's play as primarily an "inquiry" into pastoral.[1] For one of the things that stands out most clearly in reading the play together with its source is how much the pastoral atmosphere of Lodge's novel has been toned down. Rosalind and Celia buy their farm, it is true, but they do not even attempt to play at shepherd and shepherdess. The pastoral imagery, the references to the care of the flocks, the diet of cheese, that create a constant background in Lodge's novel have been dropped— even the farm itself has disappeared from view, and the two girls roam about the wood without a chore to perform, unless the producer chooses

---

[1] Bullough, *Narrative and Dramatic Sources of Shakespeare,* vol. ii, p. 153. Cf. also Muir, *Shakespeare's Sources,* vol. i, p. 62.

to give them some washing to hang on the bushes. It is true that, on the other hand, Shakespeare has developed the life of the outlaws much more fully than Lodge does, and that this life in the greenwood almost inevitably calls up for us the picture of Robin Hood. Yet Shakespeare himself has done very little to underline that picture, except for his one introductory and explanatory reference (I. i. 122). A dramatist is more tied down by his medium than a novelist; and since he had to introduce his outlaws on the stage, Shakespeare was practically compelled to sketch in a background for them with a hunting song (since he had a singer at his disposal) and a celebration of a kill; but the picture develops rather on the background of the Elizabethan chase than of the Robin Hood ballads. And as a subsummation of Renaissance types of pastoral the play fails singularly in that the most important strain, that represented by the *Arcadia*, the *Pastor Fido* and *Aminta* with their background of a pastoral state with its laws, rites and observances, is lacking. What Shakespeare has done rather is, by his introduction of the ironic commentators Jaques and Touchstone, of the yokels Audrey and William, by his realistic treatment of Corin and satirizing of Sylvius, to poke some gentle fun at the pastoral tradition, without trying to explode it altogether or even denying its basic premise of an opposition between natural kindly simplicity and the heartless sophistication of the court.

To claim, however, that the play is in the first place a good-humored skit on the pastoral idea would be to overlook other points in the treatment of the source and, above all, its position in the main line of Shakespeare's comedies, which are for the most part comedies of courtship. The skit on the pastoral exists, it is a definite element in the play; but after all, what one thinks of in the first place in connection with *As You Like It* is Orlando's wooing of the disguised Ganymede —a game that is more in earnest than he supposes—and Rosalind's attempts to enjoy the prerogatives of the courted beauty and to enforce the correct Petrarchistic attitudes on rather intractable material. Here we have that combination of the theme of love's foolishness with the clash between appearance and reality that lies at the bottom of most of Shakespeare's riper comedies and for which Lodge's novel, although it offered him ample opportunities to develop it, gave him nothing directly. In Lodge the game of wooing is the pastime of a single evening, introduced by Rosalynde to postpone her lover's departure, and it is given a serious, symbolical significance. Here Rosalynde overcomes her prudent doubts and hesitations, and surrenders herself completely to love for the first time; the lovers plight their troths, the wooing is over, and although the pretense is still kept up, the interest in the pair declines and they give place to other pairs of lovers and other courtships. For besides Rosalynde and Rosader—whose prominence is due mainly to the introductory episodes—Lodge has two other pairs of lovers, whose courtship is of equal importance. And fundamentally the love-making of all three pairs moves on the same plane of courtly, artificial sentimentality, of sighs and tears and attitudes. It is only the pains of love that interest Lodge; and as soon as one set of lovers come to an understanding, they drop into the background to make room for the next. It is only in the different acceptance of love by the women that the pairs are differentiated. Phoebe scorns love on principle—not her wooer Montanus in particular—but when she is once attacked by the disease she suffers most (since her love is unrequited), and finally makes the first advances herself. Alinda (Celia) is also something of a rebel against Cupid, but when smitten she holds back only for form's sake until she is assured of her lover's seriousness; inwardly, however, she succumbs without a struggle. Rosalynde stands halfway between the rooted enmity of the one and the gentle submissiveness of the other. She falls in love at first sight; but she has a long battle to fight within herself against the dictates of prudence and her fears of man's deceitfulness. And all through the novel, although the plot does nothing to sustain the idea, love is treated as a painful and foolish state of mind that the wise will avoid, since its fruits are bitter, and men are all deceitful, and women shallow, cruel, and fickle. For it was Lodge's intent that his readers should find, "Love anatomized by Euphues with as lively colours as in Apelles' table; roses to whip him when he is wanton, reasons to withstand him when he is wily."

That is an outlook for which Shakespeare, coming from a very different tradition, with the "true love" of ballad poetry in his mind, and the idea of marriage as a comradeship in which both sides give mutual comfort and support, as with the later Puritans, had little use. Lovers may behave foolishly, but love itself is natural and inevitable; and his Corin, instead of uttering words of warning against the tyranny of love, admits that he too has behaved foolishly in his day, and approves the folly. Rosalind may declare that lovers are all madmen who deserve to be whipped, and Jaques too is not very complimentary on the subject; but such remarks are merely a ridiculing of Lodge's attitude. Yet while accepting the follies of true love, and laughing at them, Shakespeare had little sympathy for the follies and affectations of Petrarchism. In *Love's Labour's Lost* he had punished his young men for their Petrarchistic capers, and here he preserved the Petrarchistic level of Lodge for only one pair of lovers—Phebe and Sylvius; and that pair he singles out for ridicule. Phebe with the lash of her tongue makes short work of Sylvius's imagery—the killing darts of beauty's eyes, the wounds of love (III. v. 8-27), just as Rosalind destroys the proud beauty's pretensions to lord it over her wooer. Phebe in love—

and in love out of sheer perversity, having found someone to scorn
her instead of adoring her Petrarchistically—becomes a figure of fun,
shilly-shallying between her attempts to pour scorn on the mocker
and her admiration of him. And Sylvius too is no longer the selfless
martyr of love, playing the go-between with open eyes and pleading
with Ganymede to take pity on the girl he himself loves, but a silly
dupe whom Phebe uses for her own ends. Rosalind and Orlando,
however, have been brought down to earth from their Petrarchistic
heights. Rosalind may enjoy the idea of playing the proud beauty
herself, may reproach her lover for his un-Petrarchistic cheerfulness,
plump cheeks, and neat attire, may enjoy the idea of tyrannizing over
him—her tyranny as practiced in pretense by a pert young boy is in
itself a skit on the Petrarchistic attitude. The third pair of lovers
offered no scope for a variation of treatment; Shakespeare retained the
pairing in order to provide a happy ending for Celia too; but he wasted
no space on the courting, introducing instead a fourth pair of lovers,
or rather a triangle, which in inverted form and on a lower, more
sensual plane, repeats the triangle of Phebe—Sylvius—Ganymede.
Here Touchstone, a being from another world, also comes between a
bucolic pair, and instead of bringing them together, carries off the
girl himself. And Touchstone, by his matter-of-fact, disengaged attitude to sex, provides a piquant contrast to the other lovers. But there
is also a certain piquancy in the fact—though this is not underlined
and to underline it would have introduced too harshly satirical a strain
—that Touchstone, with all his sophisticated contempt for the rustic
life, is the only one who marries into Arden, and is actually the most
flagrant example of love's blindness and waywardness. The proud
Oliver falls in love with a country wench—she is a princess in disguise.
Orlando plasters the woods with sonnets that can never reach his
beloved's eyes—but they do reach them. Like Lyly's lovers, too absorbed
in their own love-longing to recognize the same symptoms in the other,
and so unable to come to an understanding, he is too full of thoughts
of the absent Rosalind to recognize her when she is present—but he is
enabled to do his wooing without recognizing her. With these true
lovers, love's blindness actually sees further than the eyes of reason,
while Touchstone's worldly nonchalance leads him into a ridiculous
misalliance.

Thus by abandoning Lodge's moralizings and developing points
that are inherent, though undeveloped, in his plot, Shakespeare once
more achieved a complete and harmonious fusion of his two comic
themes, love's foolishness and the clash between appearance and reality.
And one might hazard the guess that what drew Shakespeare to the
novel in the first place was Orlando's blindness and the bewildering
interplay of the various planes of reality offered by Rosalind's dis-

guise, to which the stage added yet another plane, since Rosalind would be played by a boy. That perhaps and the idea of the forest of Arden, one more incorporation of that symbolical country to which the lovers retire to lose and find themselves, the park of Navarre, the moonlit wood of Athens, Illyria or the Bermuthes.[2] It is not only the fact that all Shakespeare's real invention and reorganization of plot and content is concentrated on the comedy of courtship that shows us where the chief interest of the story lay for him, and that the guying of pastoral was mainly a by-product thrown in for good measure and demanding very little brainwork on his part. The fact that the result is so very much the mixture as before confirms that interpretation.

It is not only for the increased insight into the author's intentions, however, that a study of the source is important. It also offers us a standard by which to judge, or to realize, his artistry and craftsmanship, even though the results may often be negative, i.e. show us where his specific qualities do not lie. Roughly speaking, an author's alterations in his source follow four main lines: alterations in meaning and content, such as we have been discussing, alterations in structure and plotting, in character-drawing, and in presentation or style. These lines cannot, of course, be kept strictly separate; a single alteration may easily work itself out in several ways simultaneously, so that it may be difficult or impossible to tell which was the prime motive behind it. But a scheme such as this offers a convenient basis for work.

Of Shakespeare's structural alterations in this play I have already written in a former publication.[3] They are of rather special interest, because the source is nondramatic, and yet more or less commensurate with the play, i.e. the episodes are sufficiently worked out to allow of being taken over as they are; and whatever changes have been made are probably due to the exigencies of the new dramatic form. For the most part they follow, in fact, the accepted dramaturgical traditions of the time. The popular playwrights were, many of them, aware of the theoretical demands of the learned critics, though they did not try to meet them, at least not very hard. Yet whether consciously or instinctively, their practice does show a certain approximation to those demands. Here, to sum up briefly, we may note the greater concentration and unity of the plot. The introductory history has been considerably curtailed and softened, giving an introductory act or prologue that forms a separate unit, with a rapid rise of tension up to the wrestling match, and a catastrophe—Orlando's flight; or rather, it would do, if it had not been necessary to separate the two

[2] Cf. G. K. Hunter, ed. *All's Well That Ends Well,* introduction, *New Arden Shakespeare.*

[3] "Plot Construction in Shakespeare," *Annuaire de l'université de Sofia,* Faculté Historico-philologique, t. XXXVII, 1941.

parallel scenes of the girls' banishment and Orlando's flight by a wedge scene (II. i) introducing the foresters—a fitting opening for the new act—and one preparing the way for Oliver's banishment. After that the action centers in Arden, except for one scene at court, necessary to account for Oliver's arrival, and placed at the selfsame point as in Lodge's novel, but serving also as a contrasting act-opening. The main action too is more unified in mood than with Lodge, the dangers and battles have been excised: Oliver's rescue from the lion is given in narrative only—it could hardly have been staged though it might have been altered—and the fight with the brigands is omitted altogether. Even the final revolt of the people becomes a sudden conversion of the usurper; and the unity of mood of the forest scenes is preserved.

In the same way, one may even note an approximation to unity of time in that, in accordance with the regular stage practice, all breaks in the time scheme have been omitted or glossed over. There is an obvious and inevitable interval to allow the fugitives to get to Arden, presumably another, marked by the intrusive palace scene, to let them settle down; but after that the action runs through in three consecutive days. And also there has been a further tightening of the structure through an increase of motivation—the sham wooing is introduced as a means of curing love, not merely as a pastime; and Oliver is sent to find the fugitives (for now Celia is a fugitive), not merely banished as an excuse for confiscating his estates. More important, however, is the way in which turns in the action are prepared beforehand, thus insuring a steadier flow and an effect of motivation, even if it is only apparent. The two girls are introduced through Charles's gossip of the court; and though he speaks of her uncle's affection for Rosalind, Le Beau already foresees her banishment, which in Lodge is the result of a momentary whim. And so too we know of Oliver's impending banishment well before the event. Even the sequence of Orlando's arrival in Arden is carefully, even ponderously, built up—we are shown the preparations for dinner, then the famished travellers, and only then the dinner itself with Orlando's abrupt entry. It is not perhaps surprising that this careful preparation is not used to create tension, for tension is not characteristic of comedy. Events are foreshadowed, but not so that we await them with impatience. Nor even is any tension built up round Rosalind's disguise and the possibility of its being pierced. Indeed it is not until his later plays that Shakespeare manipulates his plots to increase the dramatic tension.

The other principle behind Shakespeare's plotting, besides the achievement of a smooth, swift action without breaks or unexpected turns, is that of balance; and his most important alteration in the conduct of the story has been made to secure this. In Lodge's novel the courtship of the three couples is treated consecutively: Each one

reaches an understanding before the next usurps the interest. And
since the wooing is all on the same plane, and the preceding couples
are not lost sight of entirely, this is no great flaw—the emotional atmosphere remains the same. But Shakespeare's contrasting pairs had
to be pitted against one another continually, or else the balance would
have been destroyed. And so the Sylvius episode is brought forward
considerably and developed concurrently with the others, and so too
Touchstone and Audrey, who replace Saladyne and Alinda, are spread
out over a series of disconnected episodes running parallel with the
others. And so too the foresters, who create the atmospheric background of the play in the place of Lodge's pastoral background, are
introduced in a static, descriptive scene well before they are needed
for the plot, and are made use of in a short wedge scene (IV. ii) to
separate two of Rosalind's appearances. For neither of these two
strains has any real action been devised, nor yet for the melancholic
commentator Jaques, who weaves in and out of all the strains, drawing them more intimately together.

In this way Lodge's novel is fitted into a five-act structure, whose
divisions are given mainly through the breaks in the time scheme.
Act I covers the introduction of the novel based on the tale of Gamelyn,
though a little of this matter flows over into the second act. This too
is still preparatory, giving the arrival of the fugitives in Arden. Act III
opens with a palace scene, marking an interval of time; and it is after
that that the comedy proper begins. It occupies three days—Act III
fills one day, Act IV the morning and afternoon of the second, but
the evening, which brings the promise of the disentanglement is left
for Act V, which gives the final unravelling of the wedding. And these
five acts follow the matter of the novel fairly evenly: Act I corresponds
to 35 pages of the text (in Greg's edition [of *Rosalynde*]), Act II—
very slightly shorter—covers 27 pages; Act III—the longest of all—
brings the main plot down to p. 77, i.e., covers only 14 pages, but it has
taken in 20 pages of a later section, and actually covers 34 pages.
Act IV is the shortest, though it takes in 66 pages of the original: But
20 of these were drawn into the preceding act, while a further 15, deal-
ing with the episode of the brigands and Saladyne's wooing were
omitted, so that actually it covers 31 pages. The last act has, however,
been expanded, compared with the others, showing there was a definite
intention to make the disentanglement with its preparation fill out a
whole act: it covers only 21 pages of the novel and, though a shortish
section, is actually longer than Act IV.

These structural readjustments are comparatively slight, and more
or less routine work. They do not affect the plot at all deeply, as do
the superficially scarcely more elaborate ones in *Romeo and Juliet*.
And in the same way the general concept of the characters has scarcely

undergone any change. What alterations there are, are mainly in the reduction of romantic and improbable viciousness. The duke does not banish his own daughter in a fit of temper, as in Lodge; she runs away of her own accord, which in its turn adds to her attractiveness; and he banishes Oliver not so much in order to confiscate his lands, as to recover Celia. On the other hand, he is hostile to the whole family of de Boyes, which is what one would expect from a usurper. Oliver, too, has been somewhat improved morally; at least he is not inspired by covetousness in his hostility, and he is less underhand. He makes no pretended reconciliations—though that may be due rather to the compression of this section—nor does he actually arrange the trap of the wrestling match, though, under a certain provocation and in hot blood, he does try to make use of it to have his brother murdered, without stooping to bribery, it is true, but by means scarcely more reputable. And his next plot against Orlando's life is quite as bad as in the source. Obviously, Shakespeare was not very much intent on whitewashing his character, for it would not have been hard to invent some other motive for Orlando's flight. Nor even does he give Oliver the benefit of a spontaneous repentance in prison, as in Lodge, to make him more attractive at the end, though he does omit the ugly little touch of jealousy over his brother's apparently more successful marriage. But all these points would have been difficult to bring out on the stage; and the truth of the matter probably is that Shakespeare simply was not interested in Oliver as a character. And, with the exception of Sylvius and Phebe, whose transformation has been discussed, the other characters have been altered even less in their broad outlines. Shakespeare's characters are in general more impulsive, less under the sway of reason than Lodge's; for he has done away with all the internal debates, of which Lodge is rather fond, in which all the pros and cons of a situation are surveyed alternately—they are stilted and unconvincing in the novel; on the stage and in soliloquy they would be even worse. He has abandoned the Petrarchistic code of sighs and tears. But apart from that there is not a trait of Rosalind's character that is not to be found, in embryo at least, in her namesake. Romantic heroines, and heroes more especially, seldom have any very marked character, it is true; but Rosalind's is more marked than most. Yet almost the whole of Shakespeare's Rosalind is already contained in this speech from Lodge:

> Tush . . . art thou a woman, and hast not a sudden shift to prevent a misfortune? I, thou seest, am of a tall stature, and would very well become the person and apparel of a page; thou shalt be my mistress, and I will play the man so properly, that, trust me, in what company soever I come I will not be discovered. I will buy me a suit, and have a

rapier very handsomely at my side, and if any knave offer wrong, your page will show him the point of his weapon.[4]

And actually there is more of Shakespeare's heroine there than in the corresponding speech in Shakespeare—partly, no doubt, because in the novel she is putting on a brave front to comfort her companion whereas in the play she alone is the disconsolate one. Lodge's Rosalynde has quite a nice wit of her own, though she does not exercise it on her lover; she too thoroughly enjoys swaggering it in her man's attire, and has her relapses into womanhood; she can laugh at herself and, in spite of her Petrarchistic complaints, she can put a cheerful face on her misfortunes and meet them bravely. If anything, Shakespeare's Rosalind, because of her immediate acceptance of love at first sight, is less complex and less true to nature than Lodge's.

In fact, if anything were needed to show that the effect of a character does not really depend on the psychological makeup; that analyses of character of the type of Bradley's actually tend to sidetrack the chief critical problem; that the truth or vividness of a character depends less on the number of facets it may display and their inner harmony than on the way in which these facets are presented, the study of Rosalind and her original, because of the very simplicity of the problems involved, should serve the purpose admirably. But though it is clearly in the presentation rather than the concept of the character that Shakespeare's alchemy lies, no comparison will lay bare the process by which Lodge's lead was transmuted into gold. For Shakespeare, even while preserving the general tenor of a conversation, retains none of the details, and all the writing of the play, the naturalness, vividness, wit, and charm of the conversation, that by which his characters live and breathe, is his own creation entirely. Only here and there one can see how a slight hint from Lodge has been developed into something totally different in effect, and has generally been transferred even to a different context. Thus one may perhaps find the germ of *Under the Greenwood Tree* in Corydon's praise of the shepherd's life,[5] or of Sylvius's fugue of love (V. ii. 91 ff.) in Montanus's pleadings to Phoebe:

> My passions are many, my loves more, my thoughts loyalty, and my fancy faith: all devoted in humble devoir to the service of Phoebe; and shall I reap no reward for such fealties.[6]

If that sentence from a Euphuistic speech of nearly two pages is indeed the source of the Shakespeare passage, it shows more clearly than anything else could how little, in spite of the general similarity of the outlines, Shakespeare actually owed to Lodge.

---

[4] Greg, p. 34.
[5] Greg, p. 47.
[6] *Ibid.*, p. 119.

PART TWO

View Points

Nevill Coghill: The Basis of Shakespearian Comedy

Compared with the comedies of Shakespeare, those of Ben Jonson are no laughing matter. A harsh ethic in them yokes punishment with derision; foibles are persecuted and vices flayed; the very simpletons are savaged for being what they are. The population he chooses for his comedies in part accounts for this: it is a congeries of cits, parvenus, mountebanks, cozeners, dupes, braggarts, bullies, and bitches. No one loves anyone. If we are shown virtue in distress, it is the distress, not the virtue that matters. All this is done with an incredible, stupendous force of style.

In Shakespeare things are different. Princes and dukes, lords and ladies jostle with merchants, weavers, joiners, country sluts, friendly rogues, schoolmasters, and village policemen, hardly one of whom is incapable of a generous impulse; even a bawd may be found nursing a bastard at her own expense.

In all this it is possible to discern the promptings of two opposed temperaments; but, more objectively, we should see the operations of two different theories of comic form: for Shakespeare was not simply following the chances of temperament in designing his comedies, any more than Jonson was; each was following earlier traditions, that evolved during the Middle Ages and at the Renaissance, from the same parent stock of thought which is to be found in the writings of the Latin grammarians of the fourth century, particularly in Evanthius, Diomedes, and Donatus. . . .

Let us rearrange the commonplaces from these ragbags of analysis into the shapes that evolved from them—the Jonsonian and Shakespearian forms of Comedy, the Satiric and the Romantic. The *Satiric* concerns a middle way of life, town-dwellers, humble and private people. It pursues the principal characters with some bitterness for their vices and teaches what is useful and expedient in life and what is to be avoided. The *Romantic* expresses the idea that life is to be grasped. It is the opposite of Tragedy in that the catastrophe solves

"*The Basis of Shakespearian Comedy*," by *Nevill Coghill. From* Shakespeare Criticism, *ed. Anne Ridler (London: Oxford University Press [World Classics], 1963), pp. 201, 202, 209-10, 211. An earlier version of the essay appears in* Essays and Studies of the English Association, III *(London: John Murray, 1950). Copyright 1950 by Nevill Coghill. Reprinted by permission of the author and publisher.*

all confusions and misunderstandings by some happy turn of events. It commonly includes love-making and running off with girls. . . .

As Shakespeare matured in Comedy, he was increasingly taken with the theme of love; he may be said to have come to see it as the core of that kind. As his tragedies end in multiple death, so his comedies end in multiple marriage; and they are all marriages of mutual love, or such as we are encouraged to hope may become so. His lovers, for the most part, love at first sight, like the Lover in the *Roman de la Rose*; and like him they are *gentil*, for love is essentially an aristocratic experience; that is, an experience only possible to natures capable of refinement, be they high-born or low. In search of this refinement, Shakespeare began to imagine and explore what we have come to call his "golden world," taking a phrase of his own from *As You Like It*. He found it chiefly peopled with princes and peasants, with Courtesy and Nature in their manners. It was a world of adventure and the countryside, where Jonson's was a world of exposure and the city. The greatest adventure was love; other adventures, and misadventures, were jealousies and ficklenesses, mistaken identities, wrongly reported deaths, separations and reunions, disguises of sex and all the other improbabilities that can be fancied, entangled and at last resolved into whole harmony by some happy turn of events. It is an Eden world, but the apples are still in blossom. . . .

The definition of Comedy bequeathed to Shakespeare by the Middle Ages has a further aspect, as we have noted already, that was important to his imagination; it indicated a *narrative* structure—of adventures that would lead out of trouble into joy; this again distinguishes his Comedy from Jonson's, in whose work the story is not important; he places his characters in a situation that will display their "humours," which are like the *data* in a complex structure of argument, leading by their inner logic to some sort of Q.E.D. *Volpone* and *Epicene*, by dint of Jonson's stunning ingenuity, display their various humours in such a way as to form a story, but one can hardly say as much for *The Alchemist*; there is even less story in *Bartholomew Fair*; their powerful virtues must be found in other aspects of their composition. His characters (representing the humours indicated by their names) suffer no changes and offer no enigmas; nor should they, any more than x and y should change their values in an equation.

But Shakespeare's characters have to be changeable, for they are not fashioned to make possible a demonstration in morals, but to be credible in a world of freely imagined actions, where actions have motives other than those that fall neatly under the heading of a "humour." . . .

Peter G. Phialas: The Structure of Shakespeare's Romantic Comedies

. . . Of the components of drama, structure, theme, and character are the most important. Accordingly, the nature and mutual adjustment of these in each play form the chief subject of this study. What, in general terms, is the structure of Shakespearean romantic comedy? What sort of play is it and what is it about? In outline it follows the form of Menandrine comedy. It is nonsatiric although, as we shall see, satire as a device is indispensable to it. But here satire, instead of being the chief end, is but a means or device in a larger conception of comic structure. That structure deals with a love story which, though for a time frustrated, is in the end brought to a happy conclusion. And it nearly always includes a secondary action of strife and conflict which impinges upon and obstructs the love story but which is likewise happily resolved before the end of the play. Although these two related actions are fundamental to all Shakespearean comedy, it must be stressed again that only in the romantic comedies is the love story at the center of the action. But the similarity in structure between the Menandrine form and Shakespearean romantic comedy is to be found only in this identity of broad outline. What gives Shakespeare's romantic comedies their uniqueness is the nature of the special conflict which for a time frustrates their love stories. For in addition to the external obstruction supplied by the secondary plot, and far surpassing it in significance, there is an interior conflict, a frustration or opposition coming from the lovers themselves. It proceeds from the attitudes and resulting actions of such characters as the King and his lords in *Love's Labour's Lost,* Benedick and Beatrice, Orlando and Phebe, Orsino and Olivia, to name a few. As we shall see, the characteristic action of Shakespearean romantic comedy deals with the conflict and comic resolution of attitudes to love. One of these is the rejection of love by persons who later succumb to it; another is the sentimental idealizing of it; and a third is the realistic view of it, the concern with its physical aspect, a view generally serving to satirize and reduce the other two. Now the result of this diverting juxtaposition and comic reduction of these attitudes is two-fold: the achieving by the chief characters, whose attitudes are thus comically reduced, of a change or growth; and the emergence, stated or implied, of an ideal attitude, "ideal" here meaning the best

"The Structure of Shakespeare's Romantic Comedies." From the Introduction to Shakespeare's Romantic Comedies *by Peter G. Phialas (Chapel Hill: University of North Carolina Press, 1966), pp. xiii-xiv. Copyright © 1966 by the University of North Carolina Press. Reprinted by permission of the publisher.*

that can be hoped for in the world we know. In the early plays that ideal view is merely suggested by the juxtaposition of opposed attitudes in different characters or in the same characters at different stages in the play's action. In the later plays, particularly *As You Like It* and *Twelfth Night,* that ideal attitude is represented throughout in the temperament of the heroine. Shakespeare's achievement of a Rosalind and a Viola seems to have been a deliberate aim in the years of experimentation. It is indeed true, as Professor Frye insists, that the theme of the comic "is the integration of society, which usually takes the form of incorporating a central character into it." But in Shakespearean romantic comedy a prior and indispensable step is the integration of the individual. . . .

John S. Baxter: The Setting and Function of Comedy

. . . In the romantic comedies, then, Shakespeare does not attempt to present us with a direct criticism of life either by mirroring the affairs and doings of the world of our ordinary habitation or by creating types of the ludicrous who can in their interaction express their author's judgment upon man's behavior as a social being. For George Meredith the proper setting of comedy is the drawing room, the social world which man has created for himself; and for Meredith comedy is essentially intellectual because its function is the analysis of that artifact of man and its end is the judgment of men according to those values which man has evolved to control his group life in society. For Shakespeare the proper setting of comedy is the human spirit, the internal world of the human microcosm created by God in an act of divine love; and for Shakespeare comedy is both intellectual and emotional because its function is the enlargement of the spirit according to its God-given capacities and its end is the understanding and expressing of life as it may be lived in the light of values which man can comprehend, but which he does not properly create. Shakespearean comedy deals with man as he lives not under the law of man alone, but also under the law of nature and the law of God. This, of course, is also a description of Shakespearean tragedy. For Shakespeare does not have a tragic and comic point of view as separate and distinct things, but one set of assumptions and attitudes,

"The Setting and Function of Comedy." From "Present Mirth: Shakespeare's Romantic Comedies," by John S. Baxter, Queen's Quarterly, *LXXII (1965), 67. Copyright © 1965 by John S. Baxter. Reprinted by permission of the author and the publisher.*

one complex awareness of life, which can find expression equally in comedy and in tragedy and in the peculiarly Elizabethan combination of the two which Shakespeare sometimes permits himself.

Northrop Frye: Integrating and Isolating Tendencies in Shakespeare's Comedies

. . . The greater the emphasis on reconciliation in comedy, the more the defeated forces of the comedy tend to become states of mind rather than individuals. Shylock is the chief exception—not wholly an exception, because what is expelled is the spirit of legalism, but an exception nonetheless, and one that nearly destroys the comic mood of the play he is in. Elsewhere the individual is released from his humor and it is the humor that is expelled. In the dénouement of *The Merry Wives,* Falstaff's lust is expelled, but so are Ford's jealousy and Page's miserliness—as Falstaff says, the arrow shot at him has glanced. Hence as an individual Falstaff has as much right to be at the final party as Ford and Page have. Leontes and Posthumus are treated with the greatest indulgence as soon as they have overcome their fantasies; Claudio and Bertram eventually become quite satisfactory comic hero-husbands; the forgiveness of Angelo, Iachimo, the Antonio of *The Tempest,* the conversion of Oliver in *As You Like It,* all seem concerned to make the comic society at the end as inclusive as possible. The bad influence on Bertram in *All's Well* is said by Lafeu, and assumed by the other officers, to be Parolles; but Parolles too is an individual with a troublesome influence to be expelled.

There is, however, still a contrast between the individualizing movement of the identity of awareness and the incorporating movement of a social identity. This contrast corresponds to a split in the mind of the spectator in the audience. The comedy moves toward the crystallization of a new society; everybody, including the audience, is invited to participate in this society and in the festive mood it generates; it is usually approved by the dramatist, and the characters who obstruct it or are opposed to it are usually ridiculed. Part of us, therefore, if we like the comedy, feels involved with the new society and impelled to participate in it; but part of us will always remain a spectator, on the outside looking in. Every comic dramatist has to be aware of the ambivalence of his audience, on the alert to prevent a sudden

"Integrating and Isolating Tendencies in Shakespeare's Comedies." From A Natural Perspective, *by Northrop Frye (New York: Columbia University Press, 1965), pp. 91-92. Copyright © 1965 by Columbia University Press. Reprinted by permission of the publisher.*

unwanted alienation, as when the audience laughs in the wrong place, or an unwanted sympathy, as when it laughs too often in the right ones. Comedy . . . is a structure embodying a variety of moods, the majority of which are comic in the sense of festive or funny, but a minority of which, in any well-constructed comedy, are not. Similarly, comedy presents a group of characters, the majority of which advance toward the new society of the final scene and join it. But, again, in any well-constructed comedy there ought to be a character or two who remain isolated from the action, spectators of it, and identifiable with the spectator aspect of ourselves. . . .

Maynard Mack: Engagement and Detachment in Shakespeare's Plays

. . . That Hamlet does not manifest the extreme engagement of Othello and the rest, but seems to stand back, withholding something, a man of multiple not single directions, is perhaps the reason that our feelings about him (he is, I think, alone among the tragic heroes in this) contain no jot of patronage. He is never anyone's dupe; there are no springes he does not finally uncover. He is, in fact, partly an *eiron* figure, to use the terminology that Northrop Frye has lately restored to general circulation;[1] and his language shows it. The other heroes, hyperbolists, use the language of the *alazon*, the eiron's reversed image in the comic mirror; but Hamlet's speech is mixed. All but its most inflated resonances have an undertone of *eironeia*, the eiron's native tongue. For the most part, too, the other heroes support ironies that are thrust upon them; Hamlet, though sometimes thrust upon, knows how to return the thrust: he mines beneath the mines of others and hoists them with their own petard.

In Shakespearian comedy, the characters most sympathetic are those who, like Hamlet, combine both principles. But the total moral weight of comedy inclines generally toward the detached man, as that of tragedy inclines toward the man engaged. One is somewhat higher in the comic scale if one is Jaques, say—even though detachment, as his Seven Ages speech and his role in general show, has made him a type of

"*Engagement and Detachment in Shakespeare's Plays*," by Maynard Mack. From Essays on Shakespeare and Elizabethan Drama in Honor of Hardin Craig, ed. Richard Hosley (Columbia: University of Missouri Press, 1962; London: Routledge & Kegan Paul, Ltd., 1963), pp. 287-90. Copyright © 1962 by the Curators of the University of Missouri. Reprinted by permission of the publishers.

[1] See especially "Characterization in Shakespearean Comedy," *Shakespeare Quarterly,* IV (1953), 271-7.

comic vampire feeding curiosity on the acts and feelings of those more vital than himself—than if one is simply Silvius, engrossed by a single convention. Or again, one is higher in the scale if one is Feste than if one is the Orsino or Olivia of the opening scenes of *Twelfth Night*; if one is Puck rather than Demetrius; Costard rather than Armado; Benedick rather than Claudio. But only somewhat higher. What is really high in Shakespearian comedy is to be Rosalind, who both indulges love and schools it; Biron, who can commit himself to the folly of Navarre without failing to recognize it for what it is; Duke Theseus, who is sympathetic with imagination even while skeptical about its influence; Viola, who is man enough to please Olivia, woman enough to marry Orsino; the Benedick of the end of *Much Ado*, who has learned to eat his scoffs at love and marriage with a grin. To this group belongs notably the Fool Touchstone, who can ridicule the life of nature as wittily as the life of nurture—

> That is another simple sin in you, . . . to offer to get your living by the copulation of cattle; to be bawd to a bellwether, and to betray a she-lamb of a twelve-month to a crooked-pated old cuckoldy ram, out of all reasonable match. If thou beest not damn'd for this, the devil himself will have no shepherds—
>
> (III. ii. 82)

and who, though he sees Audrey for what she is, can accept her like a prince in a fairy tale (like Bassanio, in fact, choosing the leaden casket):

> A poor humour of mine, sir, to take that that no man else will. Rich beauty dwells like a miser, sir, in a poor house, as your pearl in your foul oyster.
>
> (V. iv. 61)

Touchstone is a good reminder that Shakespeare's plays exhibit foolery of two kinds, the dry and the sly.[2] This has often been noted, and the change from Bottom and Dogberry to Touchstone and Feste and the Fool in *Lear* credited to the replacement of Will Kempe in Shakespeare's company by Robert Armin. There is no reason to quarrel with this speculation, so long as we are aware that both styles of fooling appear in Shakespeare's plays of every date, and would almost necessarily appear there even if Armin and Kempe had never lived, for the reason that they represent the two bases of all humor, the intentional and unintentional. Dogberry's humor, obviously unintentional, is dry. It arises from an engagement to present self and present purposes so single-minded as to inhibit freedom of intellectual

[2] For an account of this contrast from a different point of view and using somewhat different terms, see W. H. Auden's valuable "Notes on the Comic," in *Thought*, XXVII (1952), 57-71, to which I am indebted.

and emotional maneuver, and its badge in Shakespearian comedy
is normally malapropism. This need not be of the glaring type
illustrated in Bottom's "There we may rehearse most obscenely and
courageously" (I. ii. 111), or Dogberry's "If I were as tedious as a
king, I could find it in my heart to bestow it all of your worship"
(III. v. 23). Juliet's Nurse manifests malapropism of a subtler kind
when, in her effort to reproduce the indignation of a great lady at
sexual insult, she drops into the treacherous idiom of: "And thou
must stand by too, and suffer every knave to use me at his pleasure!"
(II. iv. 164). Much of the humor of Mistress Quickly comes from
ringing the changes on this style of malapropism, as she walks repeatedly into semantic traps: "Thou or any man knows where to
have me, thou knave, thou!" (III. iii. 147). Still more sophisticated is
the form malapropism takes in Malvolio, who does not misuse language like Dogberry (though he does use it at least once with un-
realized equivocations—II. v. 95—like Quickly and the Nurse), but
abuses it by wrenching it, in the letter laid out for him by Maria, to
mean what he wants it to mean:

> "I may command where I adore." Why, she may command me: I serve
> her; she is my lady. Why, this is evident to any formal capacity. There
> is no obstruction in this. And the end, what should that alphabetical
> question portend? If I could make that resemble something in me!
> Softly, M, O, A, I. . . . This simulation is not as the former; and yet,
> to crush this a little, it would bow to me, for every one of these letters
> are in my name.
>
> (II. v. 126)

The deception to which Malvolio here falls victim, by "crushing"
the simulation a little, is not far different from that which victimizes
Macbeth, when he too crushes to his will the riddling speeches of the
Witches; or what King Lear allows to happen when he reads duty in
the flattering phrases of his elder daughters, ingratitude in the blunt
speaking of Cordelia; or what takes place in Othello when his whole
vocabulary begins to shift and slide, as from some hidden rock-fault,
under the erosion of Iago's insinuations. Here again the attributes of
the comic alazon and the tragic hero throw light on one another.

At the opposite pole from Dogberry's, stands Touchstone's humor,
which is intentional and "sly." It therefore has for its badge the pun,
which is a voluntary effect with language, as malapropism is involuntary. Instead of single-mindedness, pun presupposes multiple-minded-
ness; instead of preoccupation with one's present self and purposes,
an alert glance before and after; and instead of loss of intellectual and
emotional maneuverability, a gain, for language creatively used is
freedom. . . .

The intellectual action of Shakespearian comedy may frequently be read as a continuing debate between sly and dry voices, complicated, in the so-called romantic comedies, by a third voice, that of romantic convention. The pattern appears at its simplest in *A Midsummer-Night's Dream,* where the lovers speak the convention, Bottom and his companions run riot through language like those dry fools of the cinema who find themselves in a house where everything they touch comes apart in their hands, and Theseus, though no jester, shows the disengaged catholicity that belongs to "slyness." For these groups in *Much Ado* may be substituted Claudio and Hero, Dogberry and Verges, and those virtuosi of language, Beatrice and Benedick. *As You Like It* has Rosalind, Touchstone, and, within limits, Jaques, for its sly voices, Audrey and William for its dry ones, and for its convention-alists the hyperconventional Silvius and Phebe (who are themselves a species of dry fool), as well as the more moderate Celia and Orlando. *Twelfth Night's* dry fools are Aguecheek and Malvolio, who share common failings despite their differences in temperament and status and are both on the make; Feste, and in some respects Toby, Maria, and Fabian, are its sly fools; Orsino and Olivia are the conventional-ists (but again with a list toward the "dry"). . . .

Madeleine Doran: The Theme of Civilized Man

. . . This theme of civilized man, both in his own nature and in his relation to other men, is one of Shakespeare's most persistent themes, variously presented. Sometimes the terms are "nature" and "art" (as in *Love's Labour's Lost* and *The Winter's Tale*), sometimes "nature" and "nurture" (as in *The Winter's Tale, Cymbeline,* and *The Tempest*), sometimes order and disorder (as in the history plays, *Troilus and Cressida,* and *King Lear*), sometimes (as in *As You Like It, The Winter's Tale,* and *The Tempest*), the court and the "green world." But these terms are by no means interchangeable pairs; the terms alter as the focus shifts. If Shakespeare appears to be on the side of the "naturalists" against the "artsmen," he is not therefore on the side of primitive rudeness against civilization. To put him on one side or the other of any of these pairs (except order and disorder) is to miss the breadth of his vision and the depth of his perception. . . .

"The Theme of Civilized Man." From "'Yet Am I Inland Bred,'" by Madeleine Doran in Shakespeare 400: Essays by American Scholars on the Anniversary of the Poet's Birth, *ed. James G. McManaway (New York: Holt, Rinehart and Winston, 1964), p. 114. Copyright © 1964 by Holt, Rinehart and Winston, Inc. Reprinted by permission of the publisher.*

Chronology of Important Dates

	Shakespeare	The Age
1564	Shakespeare born; baptized April 26.	Marlowe born.
1582	Shakespeare married to Anne Hathaway.	
1590	Shakespeare in London; early plays.	Lodge's *Rosalynde;* Sidney's *Arcadia* (unauthorized edition); Spenser's *Faerie Queene,* Bks. I-III.
1593	*Venus and Adonis,* Shakespeare's first published work, dedicated to Earl of Southampton.	Death of Marlowe.
1594	*The Rape of Lucrece* published.	Lord Chamberlain's Company formed with Shakespeare as a sharer.
1595	*Midsummer-Night's Dream; Richard II.*	Spenser's *Amoretti;* Sidney's *Defense of Poesy* published.
1596	*Romeo and Juliet;* Hamnet, Shakespeare's only son, dies.	Spenser's *Faerie Queene,* Bks. IV-VI. *Foure Hymns,* and *Prothalamium.*
1597	*Henry IV,* Parts I and II.	Bacon's *Essays.*
1598	*Much Ado About Nothing; Merry Wives of Windsor.*	Meres' *Palladis Tamia;* Sidney's *Arcadia* (authorized, expanded version); Jonson's *Every Man in his Humour.*
1599	*Henry V; Julius Caesar; As You Like It.*	Globe Playhouse built. Spenser's death.
1600	*Twelfth Night.*	*England's Helicon.* Jonson's *Cynthia's Revels.*

Shakespeare	The Age
1603 *Hamlet,* First Quarto.	Queen Elizabeth's death; James VI of Scotland succeeds her as James I, and Lord Chamberlain's Company becomes The King's Men.
1604-8 Shakespeare's mature tragedies.	
1609-11 Late romances: *Pericles, Cymbeline, Winter's Tale, The Tempest.*	
1612 Shakespeare retires to Stratford-upon-Avon.	Webster's *The White Devil.*
1616 Shakespeare dies.	Beaumont and Cervantes die. Jonson's *Works* published in folio.
1623 Collected Plays published (First Folio).	

Notes on the Editor and Contributors

JAY L. HALIO, the editor of this volume, teaches at the University of California, Davis. He is the author of articles on contemporary literature as well as Shakespeare, and is editing *Macbeth* and *King Lear* for the Fountainwell Drama Texts.

C. L. BARBER is Professor of English at the New York State University at Buffalo and author of *Shakespeare's Festive Comedy.*

S. L. BETHELL before his death was Lecturer in English Language and Literature at the University College of South Wales and Monmouthshire. Besides *Shakespeare and the Popular Dramatic Tradition,* he wrote *The Winter's Tale: A Study.*

JOHN RUSSELL BROWN is head of the Department of Drama and Theatre Arts at Birmingham University in England, and the author of *Shakepeare's Plays in Performance.*

H. B. CHARLTON was Professor of English at the University of Manchester and wrote *Shakespearian Tragedy,* a companion volume to *Shakespearian Comedy.*

NEVILL COGHILL, a Fellow and Tutor of Exeter College for many years, was Merton Professor of English Literature at Oxford from 1957 to 1966. He is the author of *Shakespeare's Professional Skills,* and books on Chaucer and *Piers Plowman.*

MADELEINE DORAN, Professor of English at the University of Wisconsin, is the author of *Endeavors of Art* and other works.

NORTHROP FRYE, Professor of English at Victoria College, University of Toronto, is the author of *The Anatomy of Criticism, Fables of Identity,* and many other works.

HELEN GARDNER is a Fellow of St. Hilda's College, Oxford, and Merton Professor of English Literature. She has written on Eliot and Donne as well as Shakespeare, and is the author of *The Business of Criticism.*

HAROLD JENKINS, Regius Professor of Rhetoric and English Literature at the University of Edinburgh, is the author of books on Chettle and Benlowes, and *The Structural Problem in Shakespeare's Henry the Fourth.*

MAYNARD MACK, the General Editor of this series, is Professor of English and Fellow of Davenport College, Yale University. He is the author of *King Lear in Our Time,* the Twickenham Edition of Pope's *Essay on Man,* and other works on Shakespeare and Augustan literature.

MARCO MINCOFF is Professor of English, Sofia University, Bulgaria, and author of *Plot Construction in Shakespeare* and *Verbal Repetition in Elizabethan Tragedy.*

PETER G. PHIALAS teaches at the University of North Carolina, where he is Professor of English.

Selected Bibliography

Barber, C. L., *Shakespeare's Festive Comedy*. Princeton, N.J.: Princeton University Press, 1959. Discusses the "Saturnalian" pattern in Shakespeare's comedies.

Bradbrook, M. C., *Shakespeare and Elizabethan Comedy*. London: Chatto and Windus, 1951. Relates *As You Like It* to *Love's Labour's Lost* and to courtly comedy generally.

Campbell, O. J., *Shakespeare's Satire*. New York and London: Oxford University Press, 1943. Relates *As You Like It* and other plays to the background of Elizabethan satire.

Knowles, Richard, "Myth and Type in *As You Like It*," *ELH*, XXXIII (1966), 1-22. Makes much of parallels among Orlando, Hercules, and Christ.

Lascelles, Mary, "Shakespeare's Pastoral Comedy," in *More Talking of Shakespeare*, ed. John Garrett. London: Longmans, Green & Co., 1959, pp. 70-86. On the pastoral backgrounds and idea of *As You Like It*.

MacQueen, J., "*As You Like It* and the Medieval Literary Tradition," *Forum for Modern Language Studies*, I (1965), 216-29. Discusses the antithesis of Nature and Fortune, especially in Chaucer, as the medieval background for *As You Like It*.

Pettet, E. C., *Shakespeare and the Romance Tradition*. London and New York: Staples Press, 1949. Relates Shakespeare's comedies to the literature of romance and especially to the comedies of Lyly and Greene.

Smith, James, "As You Like It," *Scrutiny*, IX (1940), 9-32. Searching comparisons of Shakespeare's comedy with the tragedies, with emphasis upon Jacques' and Touchstone's functions.

Stevenson, David L., *The Love-Game Comedy*. New York: Columbia University Press, 1946. Presents Shakespeare's comedies of courtship in the historical perspective of conflicting attitudes towards love.